EASY MEDITERRANEAN DIET

COOKBOOK FOR BEGINNERS

2000+ DAYS OF SIMPLE AND DELICIOUS RECIPES FOR HEALTHY EATING

INCLUDES QUICK 30-MINUTE MEALS AND A 30-DAY MEAL PLAN FOR EVERY DAY

Norma Bellini

TABLE OF CONTENTS

INTRODUCTION

Imagine waking up every day feeling energized, light, and ready to conquer the world. Picture yourself enjoying meals that are not only delicious but also nourishing, meals that keep you full and satisfied without the guilt. If you've been struggling to find a sustainable, healthy eating plan that fits your busy life, you're not alone. Many of us are caught in the cycle of fad diets and quick fixes that leave us feeling deprived and discouraged. But what if I told you there's a way to eat that not only promotes long-term health and helps manage weight effortlessly, but also brings joy to your daily routine?

Welcome to the Mediterranean Diet Cookbook for Beginners, your gateway to a lifestyle that has stood the test of time. This book is your answer to dietary struggles and a catalyst for a healthier relationship with food. Whether you're weary of ineffective diets or seeking a more balanced and enjoyable way to eat, the Mediterranean Diet offers a sustainable, refreshing solution. With this cookbook, you'll unlock the secrets of a diet that not only nourishes your body but also delights your taste buds.

In the following chapters, you'll discover practical advice and over a hundred recipes, from breakfast to lunch to dinner, including some desserts, that make it easy to adopt the Mediterranean way of eating. You'll learn how to incorporate more vegetables, fruits, whole grains and healthy fats into your meals, making simple yet impactful changes that will benefit your health and well-being. Envision the boost in confidence you'll experience from effortlessly maintaining your weight, enhancing your energy, and relishing in nutritious, fulfilling meals.

Why should you trust the guidance in this book?
Countless individuals like you have transformed their lives with these easy, delicious, healthy meal ideas. Extensive research confirms that the Mediterranean Diet promotes health goals with its sustainable and enjoyable eating habits. Years of research and countless success stories have shown that embracing this lifestyle leads to lasting improvements in weight management, heart health, and overall well-being.

This book distills the essence of the Mediterranean way of eating into practical advice and

INTRODUCTION

recipes, making it accessible and achievable for everyone.

These recipes are quick and easy, with a focus on speed, flavour, and accessibility, helping many to improve their overall health. Rely on the well-documented benefits of the Mediterranean Diet to steer you towards a healthier lifestyle.

As you delve into the next chapter, 'The Basics of the Mediterranean Diet: A Guide to Healthy and Enjoyable Eating,' you're embarking on a journey towards a healthier, happier you. This chapter provides a thorough exploration of the fundamental principles behind the Mediterranean Diet. It will prepare you for success as you delve into the delectable recipes and useful tips. Get prepared to begin a life-changing journey that will forever alter your perspective on food and health.

THE BASICS OF THE MEDITERRANEAN DIET: A GUIDE TO HEALTHY AND ENJOYABLE EATING

The Mediterranean Diet is not just a way of eating; it is a lifestyle based on the culinary traditions of countries surrounding the Mediterranean Sea. Known for its delicious and diverse foods, this diet emphasizes whole, nutrient-rich ingredients and balanced meals. It is celebrated not only for its taste but also for its significant health benefits.

CORE COMPONENTS OF THE MEDITERRANEAN DIET

At its heart, the Mediterranean Diet focuses on consuming a variety of fresh, whole foods. The key components include:

- *Vegetables and Fruits:* Form the base of the diet and provide essential vitamins, minerals, and fibre.
- *Whole Grains:* Foods like brown rice, quinoa, and whole wheat bread are staples, offering sustained energy and digestive health.
- *Healthy Fats:* Olive oil, a central component of the diet, is loaded with monounsaturated fats that are key for maintaining heart health. Additionally, nuts and seeds provide essential fats that benefit overall wellness.
- *Lean Proteins:* Fish and seafood are preferred sources of protein, consumed several times a week. Poultry, eggs, and dairy are eaten in moderation, while red meat is limited.
- *Legumes and Nuts:* Beans, lentils, and chickpeas provide plant-based protein and fibre, making them a regular part of meals.
- *Herbs and Spices:* Herbs like basil, oregano, and thyme enhance flavour and reduce the need for salt.

7 HEALTH BENEFITS OF THE MEDITERRANEAN DIET

The Mediterranean Diet provides numerous health advantages, making it an excellent option for those aiming to enhance their overall well-being. You can rest assured that you're making a healthy choice for your body and mind.

THE BASICS OF THE MEDITERRANEAN DIET: A GUIDE TO HEALTHY AND ENJOYABLE EATING

1. *Heart Health:* Rich in healthy fats, fibre, and antioxidants, this diet reduces the risk of heart disease. Studies have shown lower levels of LDL cholesterol and improved blood vessel function among those who follow it.
2. *Weight Management:* The emphasis on whole foods and healthy fats helps with weight management by promoting satiety and reducing unhealthy cravings.
3. *Longevity:* Residents of Mediterranean areas typically enjoy longer lifespans, a benefit largely credited to their dietary habits and way of life that help lower the incidence of chronic conditions such as diabetes and cancer.
4. *Cognitive Function:* With its rich sources of antioxidants and omega-3 fatty acids, the diet bolsters brain health, which may reduce the likelihood of Alzheimer's disease and other cognitive disorders.
5. *Balancing Blood Sugar:* The Mediterranean Diet effectively manages blood sugar levels due to its emphasis on whole grains, legumes, and healthy fats, which help stabilize blood sugar and prevent spikes.
6. *Anti-Inflammatory Effects:* The diet's rich content of fruits, vegetables, nuts, and olive oil is renowned for its anti-inflammatory properties, which help decrease the risk of chronic inflammation and related illnesses.
7. *Improved Digestive Function:* Loaded with a variety of greens, juicy fruits, and hearty grains, the Mediterranean Diet enhances digestive health and prevents constipation, contributing to overall gut well-being.

INCORPORATING THE MEDITERRANEAN DIET INTO DAILY LIFE

Transitioning to the Mediterranean Diet can be seamless with a few simple changes and mindful practices.

- *Start Small:* Incorporate more vegetables into your meals. Swap refined grains for whole grains and replace butter with olive oil.

THE BASICS OF THE MEDITERRANEAN DIET: A GUIDE TO HEALTHY AND ENJOYABLE EATING

- *Plan Meals:* Create a weekly meal plan that includes a variety of foods from the core components. Focus on seasonal and fresh produce.
- *Shop Smart:* When grocery shopping, prioritize the outer aisles where fresh produce, fish, and whole grains are typically located. Avoid processed and packaged foods.
- *Cook at Home:* Cooking your meals allows you to control ingredients and portion sizes. Try grilling, roasting, and steaming to prepare foods healthily.
- *Enjoy Your Meals:* The Mediterranean Diet is as much about how you eat as what you eat. Take time to enjoy your meals, savour each bite and share food with family and friends.

EMBRACING THE MEDITERRANEAN LIFESTYLE

Beyond diet, the Mediterranean way of life includes regular physical activity and enjoying meals with others. This comprehensive strategy fosters a balanced and fulfilling life.

- *Stay Active:* Daily exercise, such as walking, cycling, or gardening, is essential for maintaining health.
- *Social Eating:* Enjoy meals with family and friends. This habit not only increases the pleasure of eating but also strengthens social bonds and supports mental health.

CONCLUSION

The Mediterranean Diet offers a path to better health and a more enjoyable way of eating. By focusing on fresh, whole foods and embracing a balanced lifestyle, you can reap the benefits of this time-tested diet. Start small, make gradual changes, and savour the journey towards a healthier, more vibrant life. Embrace the spirit of the Mediterranean—eat well, stay active, and cherish the moments shared around the table.

CHAPTER 1

BREAKFAST: ENERGIZING MORNING MEALS

Greek Yogurt Parfait with Honey and Nuts

Serves:4 | Prep Time:10 min | Cook Time:0 min

- 2 cups plain Greek yogurt
- 4 tablespoons honey (divided)
- 1 cup mixed nuts (e.g., almonds, walnuts, pistachios), roughly chopped
- 1 cup fresh berries (e.g., blueberries, strawberries, raspberries)
- 1 teaspoon vanilla extract
- 1 teaspoon ground cinnamon (optional)
- 2 tablespoons chia seeds (optional)
- Fresh mint leaves for garnish (optional)

1. Mix Yogurt: Combine Greek yogurt, vanilla extract, and 2 tablespoons honey in a bowl.
2. Layer Parfait: In serving glasses, layer yogurt, berries, and nuts. Repeat.
3. Top & Garnish: Sprinkle cinnamon and chia seeds if desired, drizzle remaining honey, and garnish with mint leaves.
4. Serve: Enjoy immediately.

Nutritional Information (per serving): Calories: 250 | Protein: 14g | Carbohydrates: 26g | Fats: 10g | Fiber: 4g | Cholesterol: 5mg | Sodium: 50mg

Health Benefits: This parfait offers protein from Greek yogurt, healthy fats from nuts, and antioxidants from berries, supporting weight loss and heart health.

Spinach and Feta Egg White Omelette

Serves:2 | Prep Time:10 min | Cook Time:10 min

- 6 large egg whites
- 1 cup fresh spinach, chopped
- 1/4 cup feta cheese, crumbled
- 1 small tomato, diced
- 1 tablespoon olive oil
- 1 clove garlic, minced
- Salt and pepper to taste
- Fresh herbs (optional): parsley, dill, or basil, chopped

1. Prep Ingredients: Chop the spinach, tomato, and any fresh herbs you wish to use.
2. Sauté Vegetables: Heat olive oil in a non-stick skillet over medium heat. Add garlic and sauté until fragrant. Add spinach and tomato, cooking until spinach is wilted.
3. Prepare Egg Whites: In a bowl, whisk egg whites with a pinch of salt and pepper.
4. Cook Omelette: Pour egg whites into the skillet over the spinach and tomato mixture. Cook until edges start to set, then sprinkle feta cheese evenly over the omelette.
5. Finish Cooking: Cover the skillet and cook for 2-3 minutes, or until the egg whites are fully set and the cheese is melted.
6. Serve: Gently fold the omelette in half and slide it onto a plate. Garnish with fresh herbs if desired.

Nutritional Information (per serving): Calories: 150 | Protein: 18g | Carbohydrates: 4g | Fats: 7g | Fiber: 1g | Cholesterol: 10mg | Sodium: 300mg

Health Benefits: This omelette provides a lean source of protein, healthy fats, and essential vitamins from spinach and tomatoes, supporting weight loss and overall health.

Mediterranean Breakfast Burrito

Serves:2 | Prep Time:10 min | Cook Time:10 min

- 4 large eggs
- 1/2 cup fresh spinach, chopped
- 1/4 cup feta cheese, crumbled
- 1/4 cup cherry tomatoes, halved
- 1/4 cup red bell pepper, diced
- 1/4 cup cucumber, diced
- 2 whole wheat tortillas
- 2 tablespoons olive oil
- 1 clove garlic, minced
- Salt and pepper to taste
- Fresh herbs (optional): parsley or dill, chopped

1. Prep Ingredients: Chop the spinach, cherry tomatoes, red bell pepper, cucumber, and any fresh herbs you wish to use.

2. Sauté Vegetables: Heat 1 tablespoon of olive oil in a non-stick skillet over medium heat. Add garlic and sauté until fragrant. Add red bell pepper and cherry tomatoes, cooking until tender.

3. Cook Eggs: In a bowl, whisk the eggs with a pinch of salt and pepper. Pour eggs into the skillet with the vegetables, and scramble until fully cooked. Remove from heat.

4. Assemble Burritos: Lay each tortilla flat and divide the cooked egg and vegetable mixture between them. Top with chopped spinach, cucumber, and crumbled feta cheese.

5. Wrap Burritos: Fold in the sides of the tortilla and then roll to form a burrito.

6. Heat Burritos: In a clean skillet, heat the remaining olive oil over medium heat. Place burritos seam-side down and cook until golden brown, about 2 minutes per side.

7. Serve: Garnish with fresh herbs if desired and serve warm.

Nutritional Information (per serving): Calories: 350 | Protein: 18g | Carbohydrates: 28g | Fats: 20g | Fiber: 6g | Cholesterol: 210mg | Sodium: 450mg

Health Benefits: This breakfast burrito offers a balanced combination of protein, healthy fats, and fiber-rich vegetables, making it a nutritious start to the day and supporting weight loss and overall health.

Quinoa Breakfast Bowl with Fresh Berries

Serves:2 | Prep Time:10 min | Cook Time:15 min

- 1 cup quinoa, rinsed
- 2 cups water
- 1 cup fresh mixed berries (e.g., blueberries, strawberries, raspberries)
- 1/2 cup almond milk (or any milk of your choice)
- 2 tablespoons honey (or maple syrup)
- 1/4 teaspoon ground cinnamon
- 1/4 teaspoon vanilla extract
- 2 tablespoons chopped nuts (e.g., almonds, walnuts, pistachios)
- 2 tablespoons chia seeds (optional)
- Fresh mint leaves for garnish (optional)

1. Cook Quinoa: In a medium saucepan, combine quinoa and water. Bring to a boil, then reduce heat to low, cover, and simmer for about 15 minutes or until the water is absorbed and quinoa is tender.

2. Mix Ingredients: Once the quinoa is cooked, stir in almond milk, honey, ground cinnamon, and vanilla extract. Mix until well combined.

Nutritional Information (per serving): Calories: 320 | Protein: 10g | Carbohydrates: 55g | Fats: 8g | Fiber: 8g | Cholesterol: 0mg | Sodium: 30mg

Health Benefits: This quinoa breakfast bowl is a great source of plant-based protein, fiber, and antioxidants from the fresh berries, supporting weight loss and overall health.

Avocado and Tomato Toast

Serves:2 | Prep Time:5 min | Cook Time:0 min

- 2 slices whole grain bread
- 1 ripe avocado
- 1 cup cherry tomatoes, halved
- 1 tablespoon olive oil
- 1 teaspoon lemon juice
- Salt and pepper to taste
- Red pepper flakes (optional)
- Fresh basil leaves for garnish (optional)

1. Toast Bread: Toast the slices of whole grain bread to your desired level of crispiness.

2. Prepare Avocado: In a bowl, mash the ripe avocado with lemon juice, salt, and pepper.

3. Assemble Toast: Spread the mashed avocado evenly over the toasted bread slices.

4. Top with Tomatoes: Place the halved cherry tomatoes on top of the avocado.

5. Drizzle and Garnish: Drizzle with olive oil and sprinkle with red pepper flakes if using. Garnish with fresh basil leaves.

Nutritional Information (per serving): Calories: 250 | Protein: 6g | Carbohydrates: 26g | Fats: 15g | Fiber: 10g | Cholesterol: 0mg | Sodium: 150mg

Health Benefits: This toast provides healthy fats from avocado, fiber from whole grain bread, and antioxidants from tomatoes, making it a nutritious choice for weight loss and overall health.

Smoked Salmon and Cucumber Bagel

Serves:2 | Prep Time:10 min | Cook Time:0 min

- 2 whole grain bagels, halved
- 4 ounces smoked salmon
- 1/2 cucumber, thinly sliced
- 1/4 cup cream cheese
- 1 tablespoon capers
- 1 tablespoon fresh dill, chopped
- 1 tablespoon lemon juice
- Salt and pepper to taste

1. Prepare Bagels: Slice the bagels in half and toast them if desired.

2. Mix Cream Cheese: In a small bowl, mix cream cheese with lemon juice, salt, and pepper.
3. Assemble Bagels: Spread the cream cheese mixture evenly on each bagel half.
4. Add Toppings: Layer smoked salmon and cucumber slices on top of the cream cheese.
5. Garnish: Sprinkle with capers and fresh dill.

Nutritional Information (per serving): Calories: 300 | Protein: 15g | Carbohydrates: 35g | Fats: 12g | Fiber: 5g | Cholesterol: 35mg | Sodium: 600mg

Health Benefits: This bagel provides lean protein from smoked salmon, healthy fats from cream cheese, and hydration from cucumber, supporting weight loss and heart health.

Lemon Ricotta Pancakes with Fresh Fruit

Serves:4 | Prep Time:10 min | Cook Time:20 min

- 1 cup ricotta cheese
- 1 cup all-purpose flour
- 1 tablespoon baking powder
- 1/4 teaspoon salt
- 2 tablespoons sugar
- 3/4 cup milk
- 2 large eggs, separated
- 1 teaspoon vanilla extract
- Zest of 1 lemon
- 2 tablespoons lemon juice
- Butter or cooking spray for the skillet
- Fresh fruit (e.g., berries, sliced bananas) for topping
- Maple syrup or honey for serving (optional)

1. Prepare Batter: In a large bowl, whisk together ricotta cheese, egg yolks, milk, vanilla extract, lemon zest, and lemon juice until smooth.
2. Mix Dry Ingredients: In another bowl, combine flour, baking powder, salt, and sugar.
3. Combine Mixtures: Gradually add dry ingredients to the wet mixture, stirring until just combined.
4. Beat Egg Whites: In a separate bowl, beat egg whites until stiff peaks form. Gently fold the egg whites into the batter.
5. Cook Pancakes: Heat a skillet or griddle over medium heat and lightly grease with butter or cooking spray. Pour 1/4 cup of batter onto the skillet for each pancake. Cook until bubbles form on the surface, then flip and cook until golden brown.
6. Serve: Top pancakes with fresh fruit and drizzle with maple syrup or honey if desired.

Nutritional Information (per serving): Calories: 280 | Protein: 12g | Carbohydrates: 34g | Fats: 11g | Fiber: 2g | Cholesterol: 115mg | Sodium: 350mg

Health Benefits: These pancakes offer a delicious combination of protein from ricotta, vitamins from fresh fruit, and the refreshing taste of lemon, promoting weight loss and overall wellness.

Mediterranean Shakshuka

Serves:4 | Prep Time:10 min | Cook Time:20 min

- 2 tablespoons olive oil
- 1 large onion, diced
- 1 red bell pepper, diced
- 3 cloves garlic, minced
- 1 teaspoon ground cumin
- 1 teaspoon ground paprika
- 1/2 teaspoon ground coriander
- 1/4 teaspoon red pepper flakes (optional)
- 1 can (28 ounces) crushed tomatoes
- Salt and pepper to taste
- 4 large eggs
- 1/4 cup crumbled feta cheese
- Fresh parsley or cilantro for garnish
- Whole grain bread or pita for serving

1. Sauté Vegetables: Heat olive oil in a large skillet over medium heat. Add diced onion and bell pepper, cooking until softened, about 5 minutes.
2. Add Spices and Garlic: Stir in garlic, cumin, paprika, coriander, and red pepper flakes (if using). Cook for 1-2 minutes until fragrant.
3. Add Tomatoes: Pour in the crushed tomatoes, season with salt and pepper, and simmer for 10 minutes until the sauce thickens.
4. Cook Eggs: Make four small wells in the sauce and crack an egg into each well. Cover the skillet and cook for 5-7 minutes until the eggs are set to your liking.
5. Garnish and Serve: Sprinkle with crumbled feta cheese and garnish with fresh parsley or cilantro. Serve with whole grain bread or pita.

Nutritional Information (per serving): Calories: 220 | Protein: 10g | Carbohydrates: 20g | Fats: 12g | Fiber: 5g | Cholesterol: 190mg | Sodium: 600mg

Health Benefits: This shakshuka provides a balanced mix of protein, healthy fats, and fibre-rich vegetables, promoting weight loss and overall health while highlighting the vibrant flavours of the Mediterranean diet.

Olive Oil and Orange Muffins

Serves:12 | Prep Time:15 min | Cook Time:20 min

- 1 3/4 cups all-purpose flour
- 1/2 teaspoon baking powder
- 1/2 teaspoon baking soda

- 1/4 teaspoon salt
- 3/4 cup granulated sugar
- 1/2 cup extra virgin olive oil
- 1/2 cup plain Greek yogurt
- 2 large eggs
- Zest of 1 orange
- 1/2 cup freshly squeezed orange juice
- 1 teaspoon vanilla extract

1. Preheat Oven: Preheat your oven to 350°F (175°C). Line a muffin tin with paper liners or grease with olive oil.
2. Mix Dry Ingredients: In a large bowl, whisk together flour, baking powder, baking soda, and salt.
3. Mix Wet Ingredients: In another bowl, combine sugar, olive oil, Greek yogurt, eggs, orange zest, orange juice, and vanilla extract. Whisk until smooth.
4. Combine Mixtures: Add the wet ingredients to the dry ingredients and stir until just combined. Do not overmix.
5. Fill Muffin Tin: Divide the batter evenly among the muffin cups, filling each about two-thirds full.
6. Bake: Bake for 18-20 minutes, or until a toothpick inserted into the center of a muffin comes out clean.
7. Cool and Serve: Allow the muffins to cool in the tin for a few minutes, then transfer to a wire rack to cool completely.

Nutritional Information (per muffin): Calories: 180 | Protein: 3g | Carbohydrates: 25g | Fats: 8g | Fiber: 1g | Cholesterol: 25mg | Sodium: 100mg

Health Benefits: These muffins provide a healthy dose of monounsaturated fats from olive oil and vitamin C from orange juice, making them a nutritious and flavorful choice for any time of day.

Fig and Almond Oatmeal

Serves:2 | Prep Time:5 min | Cook Time:10 min

- 1 cup rolled oats
- 2 cups almond milk (or any milk of your choice)
- 1/4 teaspoon ground cinnamon
- 1 tablespoon honey or maple syrup
- 4 dried figs, chopped
- 1/4 cup sliced almonds, toasted
- 1 teaspoon vanilla extract
- Fresh figs and almond slices for garnish (optional)

1.Cook Oats: In a medium saucepan, combine rolled oats, almond milk, and ground cinnamon. Bring to a boil, then reduce heat to low and simmer for 5-7 minutes, stirring occasionally, until the oats are tender and creamy.
2.Add Sweetener and Flavor: Stir in honey or maple syrup and vanilla extract. Continue to cook for another minute.
3.Mix in Figs and Almonds: Add chopped dried figs and toasted sliced almonds to the oatmeal. Stir well to combine.
4.Serve: Divide the oatmeal between two bowls. Garnish with fresh figs and additional almond slices if desired.

Nutritional Information (per serving): Calories: 300 | Protein: 8g | Carbohydrates: 50g | Fats: 9g | Fiber: 8g | Cholesterol: 0mg | Sodium: 60mg

Health Benefits: This oatmeal is rich in fiber from oats and figs, providing sustained energy and promoting digestive health, while almonds offer healthy fats and protein.

Hummus and Veggie Breakfast Wrap

Serves:2 | Prep Time:10 min | Cook Time:0 min

- 2 whole grain tortillas
- 1/2 cup hummus
- 1/2 cup baby spinach leaves
- 1/2 cucumber, thinly sliced
- 1 small carrot, grated
- 1/4 red bell pepper, thinly sliced
- 1/4 cup cherry tomatoes, halved
- 1/4 cup crumbled feta cheese
- Salt and pepper to taste
- Fresh herbs (optional): parsley or cilantro, chopped

1.Prepare Veggies: Wash and prepare all vegetables: thinly slice cucumber and red bell pepper, grate carrot, and halve cherry tomatoes.
2. Spread Hummus: Lay each tortilla flat and spread 1/4 cup hummus evenly over each.
3. Layer Veggies: Top with baby spinach leaves, cucumber slices, grated carrot, red bell pepper, and cherry tomatoes.
4. Add Feta and Season: Sprinkle crumbled feta cheese over the veggies. Season with salt and pepper to taste.
5. Roll Wraps: Roll up the tortillas tightly, folding in the sides as you go.
6. Serve: Slice each wrap in half and serve immediately. Garnish with fresh herbs if desired.

Nutritional Information (per serving): Calories: 250 | Protein: 8g | Carbohydrates: 30g | Fats: 10g | Fiber: 6g | Cholesterol: 15mg | Sodium: 400mg

Health Benefits: This breakfast wrap combines fiber-rich vegetables with plant-based protein from hummus and healthy fats from olive oil, supporting weight loss and providing sustained energy.

Pesto and Egg Breakfast Pizza

Serves:2 | Prep Time:10 min | Cook Time:15 min

- 1 whole grain pizza crust (pre-made or homemade)
- 1/2 cup pesto sauce
- 1 cup baby spinach leaves
- 1/2 cup cherry tomatoes, halved
- 1/4 cup crumbled feta cheese
- 2 large eggs
- Salt and pepper to taste
- Fresh basil leaves for garnish (optional)

1. Preheat Oven: Preheat your oven to 425°F (220°C).
2. Prepare Pizza Base: Place the whole grain pizza crust on a baking sheet or pizza stone.
3. Spread Pesto: Evenly spread the pesto sauce over the pizza crust.
4. Add Toppings: Top with baby spinach leaves, cherry tomatoes, and crumbled feta cheese.
5. Add Eggs: Carefully crack one egg onto each half of the pizza, keeping the yolk intact.
6. Bake: Bake in the preheated oven for 12-15 minutes, or until the egg whites are set and the yolks are still slightly runny.
7. Season and Garnish: Remove from the oven, season with salt and pepper, and garnish with fresh basil leaves if desired.
8. Serve: Slice and serve immediately.

Nutritional Information (per serving): Calories: 350 | Protein: 15g | Carbohydrates: 30g | Fats: 18g | Fiber: 4g | Cholesterol: 200mg | Sodium: 600mg

Health Benefits: This breakfast pizza combines the protein and healthy fats from eggs and pesto with fiber-rich whole grains and vegetables, making it a balanced and nutritious meal to start your day.

Greek Yogurt and Granola Parfait

Serves:2 | Prep Time:5 min | Cook Time:0 min

- 2 cups plain Greek yogurt
- 1 cup granola
- 1 cup fresh berries (e.g., blueberries, strawberries, raspberries)
- 2 tablespoons honey or maple syrup
- 1 teaspoon vanilla extract
- Fresh mint leaves for garnish (optional)

1. Prepare Yogurt: In a bowl, mix Greek yogurt with vanilla extract.
2. Layer Parfait: In serving glasses, layer 1/2 cup yogurt, followed by 1/4 cup granola, and 1/4 cup fresh berries. Repeat layers.
3. Top and Drizzle: Top with remaining yogurt and berries. Drizzle with honey or maple syrup.
4. Garnish: Garnish with fresh mint leaves if desired.

Nutritional Information (per serving): Calories: 350 | Protein: 15g | Carbohydrates: 50g | Fats: 10g | Fiber: 5g | Cholesterol: 0mg | Sodium: 150mg

Health Benefits: This parfait provides a balanced mix of protein from Greek yogurt, fiber from granola, and antioxidants from fresh berries, making it a nutritious and delicious start to your day.

Sun-Dried Tomato and Spinach Frittata

Serves:4 | Prep Time:10 min | Cook Time:20 min

- 8 large eggs
- 1/4 cup milk (optional)
- 1/2 cup sun-dried tomatoes, chopped
- 2 cups fresh spinach, chopped
- 1/2 cup feta cheese, crumbled
- 1 small onion, finely chopped
- 2 cloves garlic, minced
- 2 tablespoons olive oil
- Salt and pepper to taste
- Fresh basil leaves for garnish (optional)

1. Preheat Oven: Preheat your oven to 375°F (190°C).
2. Sauté Onions and Garlic: In an oven-safe skillet, heat olive oil over medium heat. Add onion and garlic, cooking until softened.
3. Add Spinach and Tomatoes: Stir in chopped spinach and sun-dried tomatoes. Cook until spinach is wilted.
4. Prepare Egg Mixture: In a bowl, whisk together eggs, milk (if using), salt, and pepper.
5. Combine and Cook: Pour the egg mixture over the vegetables in the skillet. Sprinkle with crumbled feta cheese.
6. Bake Frittata: Transfer the skillet to the preheated oven and bake for 15-20 minutes, or until the eggs are set and the top is golden.
7. Serve: Garnish with fresh basil leaves if desired. Slice and serve warm.

Nutritional Information (per serving): Calories: 250 | Protein: 14g | Carbohydrates: 6g | Fats: 18g | Fiber: 2g | Cholesterol: 285mg | Sodium: 400mg

Health Benefits: This frittata offers a nutritious combination of protein from eggs, vitamins from spinach, and healthy fats from olive oil, making it a balanced and delicious meal to support overall health and weight management

Chickpea Flour Breakfast Crepes

Serves:4 | Prep Time:10 min | Cook Time:20 min

- 1 cup chickpea flour (also known as besan or gram flour)
- 1 1/4 cups water
- 2 tablespoons olive oil
- 1/4 teaspoon salt
- 1/4 teaspoon turmeric (optional)
- 1/2 teaspoon cumin powder (optional)
- Fresh herbs (optional): parsley, cilantro, or chives, chopped
- Toppings: Fresh vegetables (e.g., spinach, tomatoes, cucumbers), avocado slices, or your choice of protein (e.g., smoked salmon, scrambled eggs)

1. Prepare Batter: In a mixing bowl, whisk together chickpea flour, water, olive oil, salt, turmeric, and cumin powder until smooth. If using fresh herbs, stir them into the batter.
2. Rest Batter: Let the batter rest for 5-10 minutes to allow the flour to absorb the water.
3. Heat Skillet: Heat a non-stick skillet over medium heat. Lightly grease with a small amount of olive oil.
4. Cook Crepes: Pour a ladleful of batter into the skillet, swirling to spread it evenly into a thin layer. Cook for 2-3 minutes until the edges lift slightly and the bottom is golden brown. Flip and cook for another 1-2 minutes.
5. Repeat: Repeat with the remaining batter, greasing the skillet as needed.
6. Serve: Fill each crepe with your choice of toppings and fold or roll them up.

Nutritional Information (per serving): Calories: 150 | Protein: 6g | Carbohydrates: 20g | Fats: 5g | Fiber: 3g | Cholesterol: 0mg | Sodium: 150mg

Health Benefits: These chickpea flour crepes are gluten-free, high in protein and fiber, and provide a nutritious base for a variety of healthy fillings, supporting weight loss and overall well-being.

CHAPTER 2

SNACKS AND APPETIZERS - HEALTHY AND TASTY SNACKS

Tzatziki with Pita Chips

Serves:4 | Prep Time:15 min | Cook Time:10 min

For the Tzatziki:
- 1 cup Greek yogurt
- 1/2 cucumber, grated and excess water squeezed out
- 2 cloves garlic, minced
- 1 tablespoon olive oil
- 1 tablespoon fresh lemon juice
- 1 tablespoon fresh dill, chopped (or 1 teaspoon dried dill)
- Salt and pepper to taste

For the Pita Chips:
- 4 whole wheat pitas
- 2 tablespoons olive oil
- 1/2 teaspoon dried oregano
- 1/2 teaspoon garlic powder
- Salt to taste

1. Prepare Tzatziki: In a medium bowl, combine Greek yogurt, grated cucumber, minced garlic, olive oil, lemon juice, dill, salt, and pepper. Mix well. Cover and refrigerate for at least 15 minutes to allow the flavors to meld.

2. Prepare Pita Chips:
- Preheat oven to 375°F (190°C).
- Cut each pita into 8 wedges. Place on a baking sheet.
- In a small bowl, mix olive oil, dried oregano, garlic powder, and salt. Brush pita wedges with the olive oil mixture.
- Bake for 10 minutes, or until crispy and golden brown. Remove from oven and let cool.

3. Serve: Transfer the tzatziki to a serving bowl. Arrange the pita chips around the tzatziki.

Nutritional Information (per serving): Calories: 180 | Protein: 5g | Carbohydrates: 20g | Fats: 9g | Fiber: 3g | Cholesterol: 0mg | Sodium: 200mg

Health Benefits:
This snack provides protein and probiotics from Greek yogurt, healthy fats from olive oil, and whole grains from pita, making it a nutritious and satisfying option.

Stuffed Grape Leaves (Dolmas)

Serves:6 | Prep Time:20 min | Cook Time:30 min

- 1 jar (16 oz) grape leaves, rinsed and drained
- 1 cup rice, uncooked
- 1 small onion, finely chopped
- 1/4 cup pine nuts
- 1/4 cup currants or raisins
- 2 tbsp olive oil
- 2 tbsp lemon juice
- 2 tbsp fresh dill, chopped
- 2 tbsp fresh mint, chopped
- 1 tsp salt
- 1/2 tsp black pepper
- 2 cups water or vegetable broth

1.In a medium saucepan, heat 1 tbsp olive oil over medium heat. Add the chopped onion and sauté until translucent.

2. Stir in the rice, pine nuts, currants, dill, mint, salt, and black pepper. Cook for 2-3 minutes, stirring frequently.

3. Add 1 cup of water or vegetable broth and bring to a boil. Reduce heat, cover, and simmer until the liquid is absorbed and the rice is partially cooked, about 10 minutes. Let cool slightly.

4. Lay a grape leaf flat, shiny side down. Place a spoonful of the rice mixture in the center and fold the sides over the filling, then roll up tightly.

5. Repeat with the remaining grape leaves and filling.

6. Place the stuffed grape leaves seam-side down in a large pot. Drizzle with the remaining olive oil and lemon juice.

7. Add the remaining water or vegetable broth to the pot. Cover and simmer over low heat for 30 minutes, or until the grape leaves are tender.

8. Serve warm or cold.

Nutritional Information (per serving): Calories: 150 | Protein: 3g | Carbohydrates: 20g | Fats: 7g | Fiber: 3g | Cholesterol: 0mg | Sodium: 300mg

Health Benefits: Stuffed Grape Leaves are a flavorful and healthy appetizer rich in antioxidants and fiber, promoting digestive health and overall wellness.

Olive Tapenade Crostini

Serves:6 | Prep Time:10 min | Cook Time:10 min

- 1 cup Kalamata olives, pitted
- 1/4 cup green olives, pitted
- 2 cloves garlic
- 2 tbsp capers, drained
- 2 tbsp fresh parsley
- 2 tbsp lemon juice
- 1/4 cup olive oil
- 1 baguette, sliced
- Fresh basil leaves (for garnish)

1. Preheat your oven to 400°F (200°C).
2. In a food processor, combine the Kalamata olives, green olives, garlic, capers, parsley, and lemon juice. Pulse until finely chopped.
3. With the processor running, slowly add the olive oil until the mixture is well combined but still slightly chunky.
4. Place the baguette slices on a baking sheet and toast in the preheated oven for 5-7 minutes or until golden brown.
5. Spread the olive tapenade on the toasted baguette slices.
6. Garnish with fresh basil leaves before serving.

Nutritional Information (per serving): Calories: 150 | Protein: 3g | Carbohydrates: 15g | Fats: 9g | Fiber: 2g | Cholesterol: 0mg | Sodium: 400mg

Health Benefits: Olive Tapenade Crostini is a savory and healthy appetizer rich in healthy fats and antioxidants, promoting heart health and overall wellness. The combination of olives, capers, and olive oil provides essential vitamins and minerals, aligning with the Mediterranean Diet's emphasis on fresh, nutritious ingredients.

Caprese Skewers

Serves:6 | Prep Time:10 min | Cook Time:0 min

- 24 cherry tomatoes
- 24 fresh basil leaves
- 24 mini mozzarella balls (bocconcini)
- 2 tbsp balsamic glaze
- 2 tbsp olive oil

1. Thread one cherry tomato, one basil leaf, and one mozzarella ball onto each skewer. Repeat until all ingredients are used.
2. Arrange the skewers on a serving platter.
3. Drizzle with balsamic glaze and olive oil.
4. Serve immediately.

Nutritional Information (per serving): Calories: 100 | Protein: 5g | Carbohydrates: 3g | Fats: 8g | Fiber: 1g | Cholesterol: 15mg | Sodium: 150mg

Health Benefits: Caprese Skewers are a fresh and nutritious appetizer rich in antioxidants, healthy fats, and protein, promoting heart health and overall wellness. The combination of cherry tomatoes, basil, and mozzarella provides essential vitamins and minerals, aligning with the Mediterranean Diet's emphasis on fresh, nutritious ingredients.

Spicy Marinated Olives

Serves:4 | Prep Time:10 min | Cook Time:0 min

- 2 cups mixed olives (green and black), pitted
- 1/4 cup extra virgin olive oil
- 2 cloves garlic, minced
- 1 tablespoon lemon zest
- 1 tablespoon fresh lemon juice
- 1 teaspoon crushed red pepper flakes
- 1 teaspoon dried oregano
- 1 teaspoon smoked paprika
- 1 teaspoon ground cumin
- 1/2 teaspoon black pepper
- 1/4 cup fresh parsley, chopped

1. Combine Ingredients: In a large bowl, mix together the olive oil, minced garlic, lemon zest, lemon juice, crushed red pepper flakes, oregano, smoked paprika, ground cumin, and black pepper.
2. Marinate Olives: Add the olives to the bowl and toss to coat them evenly with the marinade. Cover and refrigerate for at least 2 hours, preferably overnight, to allow the flavours to develop.
3. Serve: Before serving, let the olives come to room temperature and stir in the fresh parsley. Transfer to a serving dish and enjoy.

Nutritional Information (per serving): Calories: 150 | Protein: 1g | Carbohydrates: 4g | Fats: 14g | Fiber: 2g | Cholesterol: 0mg | Sodium: 400mg

Health Benefits: These spicy marinated olives provide healthy monounsaturated fats, antioxidants from olive oil, and anti-inflammatory properties from spices, making them a nutritious and flavorful snack.

Baked Falafel Bites

Serves:4 | Prep Time:15 min | Cook Time:20 min

- 1 can (15 ounces) chickpeas, drained and rinsed
- 1/2 cup fresh parsley, chopped
- 1/2 cup fresh cilantro, chopped
- 1 small onion, finely chopped
- 3 cloves garlic, minced
- 2 tablespoons all-purpose flour (or chickpea flour for gluten-free)
- 1 teaspoon ground cumin
- 1 teaspoon ground coriander
- 1/2 teaspoon baking powder
- 1/2 teaspoon salt
- 1/4 teaspoon black pepper
- 2 tablespoons olive oil

1. Preheat Oven: Preheat your oven to 375°F (190°C). Line a baking sheet with parchment paper or lightly grease with olive oil.
2. Prepare Falafel Mixture: In a food processor, combine chickpeas, parsley, cilantro, onion, garlic, flour, cumin, coriander, baking powder, salt, and pepper. Pulse until the mixture is well combined but still slightly chunky. Do not over-process.
3. Form Falafel Bites: Scoop out tablespoon-sized portions of the mixture and shape them into small balls or patties. Place them on the prepared baking sheet.
4. Bake Falafel Bites: Brush the falafel bites with olive oil. Bake in the preheated oven for 20 minutes, flipping halfway through, until golden brown and crispy.
5. Serve: Serve warm with tzatziki, hummus, or your favorite dipping sauce.

Nutritional Information (per serving): Calories: 180 | Protein: 6g | Carbohydrates: 20g | Fats: 8g | Fiber: 5g | Cholesterol: 0mg | Sodium: 350mg

Health Benefits:
These baked falafel bites are rich in plant-based protein and fiber, providing a nutritious and satisfying snack or appetizer that supports weight loss and overall health.

Cucumber Feta Rolls

Serves:4 | Prep Time:15 min | Cook Time:0 min

- 2 large cucumbers
- 1/2 cup feta cheese, crumbled
- 1/4 cup Greek yogurt
- 1 tablespoon olive oil
- 1 tablespoon fresh dill, chopped
- 1 tablespoon fresh lemon juice
- 1 clove garlic, minced
- Salt and pepper to taste
- Fresh dill or parsley for garnish (optional)

1. Prepare Cucumbers: Use a vegetable peeler or mandoline to slice the cucumbers lengthwise into thin strips.
2. Make Feta Filling: In a bowl, mix together feta cheese, Greek yogurt, olive oil, dill, lemon juice, minced garlic, salt, and pepper until well combined.
3. Assemble Rolls: Place a small spoonful of the feta mixture at one end of each cucumber strip. Roll up the cucumber slices around the filling and secure with a toothpick if needed.
4. Garnish and Serve: Arrange the cucumber rolls on a serving platter and garnish with fresh dill or parsley if desired. Serve immediately.

Nutritional Information (per serving): Calories: 100 | Protein: 4g | Carbohydrates: 5g | Fats: 7g | Fiber: 1g | Cholesterol: 15mg | Sodium: 200mg

Health Benefits:
These cucumber feta rolls are a refreshing and low-calorie snack, rich in protein from Greek yogurt and feta, and hydrating and fiber-rich from cucumbers, supporting weight loss and overall health.

Roasted Garlic and White Bean Dip

Serves:4 | Prep Time:10 min | Cook Time:30 min

- 1 head of garlic
- 2 tablespoons olive oil (divided)
- 1 can (15 ounces) cannellini beans, drained and rinsed
- 1/4 cup fresh lemon juice
- 1/4 cup water
- 1 tablespoon tahini
- 1 teaspoon ground cumin
- Salt and pepper to taste
- Fresh parsley for garnish (optional)
- Vegetables or pita chips for serving

1. Roast Garlic: Preheat your oven to 400°F (200°C). Slice the top off the head of garlic to expose the cloves.

Drizzle with 1 tablespoon of olive oil, wrap in foil, and roast for 30 minutes or until the cloves are soft and golden.

2. Prepare Dip: Once the garlic is cool enough to handle, squeeze the roasted cloves out of their skins into a food processor. Add the cannellini beans, lemon juice, water, tahini, remaining olive oil, ground cumin, salt, and pepper.

3. Blend: Process the mixture until smooth and creamy. If the dip is too thick, add a bit more water or olive oil to reach the desired consistency.

4. Serve: Transfer the dip to a serving bowl, garnish with fresh parsley if desired, and serve with fresh vegetables or pita chips.

Nutritional Information (per serving): Calories: 180 | Protein: 6g | Carbohydrates: 20g | Fats: 8g | Fiber: 5g | Cholesterol: 0mg | Sodium: 200mg

Health Benefits:
This white bean dip is rich in plant-based protein and fiber from the beans and healthy fats from olive oil, making it a nutritious and satisfying snack that supports weight loss and overall health.

Grilled Halloumi with Lemon

Serves:4 | Prep Time:5 min | Cook Time:10 min

- 8 ounces halloumi cheese, sliced into 1/4-inch thick pieces
- 2 tablespoons olive oil
- Juice of 1 lemon
- Freshly ground black pepper to taste
- Fresh herbs for garnish (optional): parsley, mint, or dill

1. Prepare Halloumi: Preheat a grill or grill pan over medium-high heat. Brush the halloumi slices with olive oil on both sides.

2. Grill Cheese: Place the halloumi on the grill and cook for 2-3 minutes on each side, until grill marks appear and the cheese is golden brown and slightly softened.

3. Add Lemon and Pepper: Remove the grilled halloumi from the grill and place on a serving platter. Drizzle with lemon juice and sprinkle with freshly ground black pepper.

4. Garnish and Serve: Garnish with fresh herbs if desired and serve immediately.

Nutritional Information (per serving): Calories: 200 | Protein: 12g | Carbohydrates: 2g | Fats: 16g | Fiber: 0g | Cholesterol: 25mg | Sodium: 600mg

Health Benefits:
Grilled halloumi provides a good source of protein and calcium, while the addition of olive oil and lemon juice enhances the flavors and adds heart-healthy fats and vitamin C, making it a delicious and nutritious appetizer.

Mediterranean Stuffed Mini Peppers

Serves:4 | Prep Time:15 min | Cook Time:15 min

- 12 mini bell peppers
- 1 cup cooked quinoa
- 1/2 cup feta cheese, crumbled
- 1/4 cup sun-dried tomatoes, chopped
- 1/4 cup Kalamata olives, chopped
- 2 tablespoons pine nuts, toasted
- 2 tablespoons fresh parsley, chopped
- 1 tablespoon olive oil
- 1 tablespoon lemon juice
- Salt and pepper to taste

1. Preheat Oven: Preheat your oven to 375°F (190°C).

2. Prepare Peppers: Slice the tops off the mini bell peppers and remove the seeds. Arrange them on a baking sheet.

3. Make Filling: In a bowl, combine cooked quinoa, feta cheese, sun-dried tomatoes, Kalamata olives, toasted pine nuts, fresh parsley, olive oil, lemon juice, salt, and pepper. Mix well.

4. Stuff Peppers: Spoon the quinoa mixture into each mini bell pepper, filling them to the top.

5. Bake: Bake in the preheated oven for 15 minutes or until the peppers are tender and the filling is heated through.

6. Serve: Arrange the stuffed mini peppers on a serving platter and enjoy warm.

Nutritional Information (per serving): Calories: 180 | Protein: 6g | Carbohydrates: 16g | Fats: 10g | Fiber: 3g | Cholesterol: 15mg | Sodium: 300mg

Health Benefits: These stuffed mini peppers are packed with protein, fiber, and healthy fats from quinoa, feta, and olives, providing a nutritious and flavorful snack that supports weight loss and overall health.

Zucchini Fritters with Tzatziki

Serves:4 | Prep Time:20 min | Cook Time:15 min

For the Zucchini Fritters:
- 4 medium zucchinis, grated
- 1 teaspoon salt
- 1/2 cup all-purpose flour (or chickpea flour for gluten-free)
- 2 large eggs, beaten
- 1/4 cup scallions, finely chopped
- 2 cloves garlic, minced
- 1/4 cup fresh dill, chopped
- 1/4 teaspoon black pepper
- 2 tablespoons olive oil (for frying)

For the Tzatziki Sauce:
- 1 cup Greek yogurt
- 1/2 cucumber, grated and excess water squeezed out
- 2 cloves garlic, minced
- 1 tablespoon olive oil

- 1 tablespoon fresh lemon juice
- 1 tablespoon fresh dill, chopped
- Salt and pepper to taste

1. Prepare Zucchini: Grate the zucchini and place them in a colander. Sprinkle with salt and let sit for 10 minutes to draw out excess moisture. Squeeze out as much liquid as possible using a clean kitchen towel or cheesecloth.
2. Make Fritter Batter: In a large bowl, combine the grated zucchini, flour, beaten eggs, scallions, garlic, dill, and black pepper. Mix well until all ingredients are incorporated.
3. Cook Fritters: Heat olive oil in a large skillet over medium heat. Scoop about 2 tablespoons of the zucchini mixture for each fritter and drop it into the skillet, flattening slightly with a spatula. Cook for 3-4 minutes on each side or until golden brown and crispy. Transfer to a paper towel-lined plate to drain excess oil.
4. Prepare Tzatziki Sauce: In a bowl, combine Greek yogurt, grated cucumber, garlic, olive oil, lemon juice, dill, salt, and pepper. Mix well and refrigerate until ready to serve.
5. Serve: Serve the zucchini fritters warm with a side of tzatziki sauce for dipping.

Nutritional Information (per serving): Calories: 220 | Protein: 8g | Carbohydrates: 18g | Fats: 14g | Fiber: 2g | Cholesterol: 70mg | Sodium: 400mg

Health Benefits: These zucchini fritters are a nutritious and tasty way to enjoy vegetables, providing fiber, vitamins, and healthy fats, while the tzatziki sauce adds protein and probiotics from Greek yogurt, supporting digestive health and weight management.

Herbed Goat Cheese Spread

Serves:4 | Prep Time:10 min | Cook Time:0 min

- 8 ounces goat cheese, softened
- 2 tablespoons olive oil
- 1 tablespoon fresh lemon juice
- 1 tablespoon fresh dill, chopped
- 1 tablespoon fresh parsley, chopped
- 1 tablespoon fresh chives, chopped
- 1 teaspoon fresh thyme leaves
- 1 clove garlic, minced
- Salt and pepper to taste
- Fresh vegetables, crackers, or bread for serving

1. Mix Ingredients: In a medium bowl, combine softened goat cheese, olive oil, lemon juice, dill, parsley, chives, thyme, and minced garlic. Mix well until smooth and creamy.
2. Season: Add salt and pepper to taste. Adjust seasoning if necessary.
3. Serve: Transfer the herbed goat cheese spread to a serving dish. Serve with fresh vegetables, crackers, or bread.

Nutritional Information (per serving): Calories: 200 | Protein: 7g | Carbohydrates: 2g | Fats: 18g | Fiber: 1g | Cholesterol: 25mg | Sodium: 150mg

Health Benefits: This herbed goat cheese spread provides healthy fats from olive oil and goat cheese, along with a burst of fresh herbs that offer vitamins and antioxidants, making it a delicious and nutritious appetizer option.

Chickpea and Avocado Toast

Serves:2 | Prep Time:10 min | Cook Time:0 min

- 2 slices whole grain bread
- 1 ripe avocado
- 1/2 cup canned chickpeas, drained and rinsed
- 1 tablespoon olive oil
- 1 tablespoon lemon juice
- 1/4 teaspoon cumin
- Salt and pepper to taste
- Red pepper flakes (optional)
- Fresh herbs for garnish (optional): parsley, cilantro, or chives

1. Toast Bread: Toast the slices of whole grain bread to your desired level of crispiness.
2. Prepare Avocado Mixture: In a bowl, mash the ripe avocado with a fork. Add lemon juice, cumin, salt, and pepper, mixing well.
3. Prepare Chickpeas: In another bowl, lightly mash the chickpeas with a fork. Mix with olive oil, salt, and pepper.
4. Assemble Toast: Spread the mashed avocado mixture evenly over each slice of toasted bread. Top with mashed chickpeas.
5. Garnish: Sprinkle with red pepper flakes and fresh herbs if desired.
6. Serve: Enjoy immediately.

Nutritional Information (per serving): Calories: 250 | Protein: 7g | Carbohydrates: 28g | Fats: 13g | Fiber: 10g | Cholesterol: 0mg | Sodium: 220mg

Health Benefits:
This chickpea and avocado toast is rich in fiber, healthy fats, and plant-based protein, making it a nutritious and satisfying snack that supports weight loss and overall health.

Tomato and Basil Bruschetta

Serves:4 | Prep Time:10 min | Cook Time:5 min

- 4 slices of whole grain baguette or crusty bread
- 2 cups cherry tomatoes, diced
- 2 cloves garlic, minced
- 1/4 cup fresh basil leaves, chopped
- 2 tablespoons olive oil
- 1 tablespoon balsamic vinegar
- Salt and pepper to taste
- Extra basil leaves for garnish (optional)

1. Prepare Bread: Preheat your oven or toaster oven to 375°F (190°C). Arrange the bread slices on a baking sheet and toast for about 5 minutes, or until golden and crispy.
2. Prepare Tomato Mixture: In a bowl, combine diced cherry tomatoes, minced garlic, chopped basil, olive oil, balsamic vinegar, salt, and pepper. Mix well.
3. Assemble Bruschetta: Spoon the tomato mixture evenly over the toasted bread slices.
4. Garnish and Serve: Garnish with extra basil leaves if desired and serve immediately.

Nutritional Information (per serving): Calories: 150 | Protein: 4g | Carbohydrates: 20g | Fats: 7g | Fiber: 3g | Cholesterol: 0mg | Sodium: 200mg

Health Benefits: This bruschetta is a fresh and light appetizer rich in vitamins from tomatoes and basil, healthy fats from olive oil, and fiber from whole grain bread, making it a nutritious and delicious option for any occasion.

CHAPTER 3

BEANS AND GRAINS - NUTRIENT-RICH PLANT PROTEINS

Lemon Garlic Chickpeas

Serves:4 | Prep Time:10 min | Cook Time:10 min

- 2 cans (15 ounces each) chickpeas, drained and rinsed
- 3 tablespoons olive oil
- 3 cloves garlic, minced
- Zest and juice of 1 lemon
- 1 teaspoon ground cumin
- 1/2 teaspoon paprika
- Salt and pepper to taste
- 2 tablespoons fresh parsley, chopped (optional)

1. Heat Oil: In a large skillet, heat olive oil over medium heat.
2. Cook Garlic: Add minced garlic and sauté for about 1 minute until fragrant.
3. Add Chickpeas: Stir in the chickpeas, lemon zest, lemon juice, ground cumin, paprika, salt, and pepper. Cook, stirring frequently, for about 5-7 minutes until chickpeas are heated through and slightly crispy.
4. Garnish and Serve: Remove from heat and stir in chopped parsley if using. Serve warm.

Nutritional Information (per serving): Calories: 220 | Protein: 8g | Carbohydrates: 26g | Fats: 10g | Fiber: 7g | Cholesterol: 0mg | Sodium: 300mg

Health Benefits: These lemon garlic chickpeas are rich in plant-based protein and fiber, providing a flavorful and nutritious dish that supports weight loss and overall health.

Farro Salad with Roasted Vegetables

Serves:4 | Prep Time:15 min | Cook Time:30 min

- 1 cup farro
- 2 cups water or vegetable broth
- 1 red bell pepper, diced
- 1 zucchini, diced
- 1 red onion, diced
- 1 cup cherry tomatoes, halved
- 3 tablespoons olive oil (divided)
- 1 teaspoon dried oregano
- Salt and pepper to taste
- 1/4 cup feta cheese, crumbled
- 2 tablespoons fresh parsley, chopped
- 1 tablespoon balsamic vinegar

1. Cook Farro: In a medium saucepan, bring water or vegetable broth to a boil. Add farro, reduce heat to low, cover, and simmer for about 20-25 minutes until tender. Drain any excess liquid and set aside to cool.
2. Preheat Oven: Preheat your oven to 400°F (200°C).
3. Roast Vegetables: On a baking sheet, toss red bell pepper, zucchini, red onion, and cherry tomatoes with 2 tablespoons of olive oil, dried oregano, salt, and pepper. Roast for about 20-25 minutes until tender and slightly caramelized.
4. Combine Salad: In a large bowl, combine cooked farro, roasted vegetables, feta cheese, and fresh parsley.
5. Dress Salad: Drizzle with the remaining 1 tablespoon of olive oil and balsamic vinegar. Toss gently to combine.
6. Serve: Serve the salad warm or at room temperature.

Nutritional Information (per serving): Calories: 250 | Protein: 8g | Carbohydrates: 36g | Fats: 10g | Fiber: 7g | Cholesterol: 10mg | Sodium: 300mg

Health Benefits: This farro salad is packed with fiber, protein, and vitamins from whole grains and roasted vegetables, making it a nutritious and satisfying dish that supports weight loss and overall health.

Lentil and Tomato Stew

Serves:4 | Prep Time:10 min | Cook Time:30 min

- 1 cup dried lentils, rinsed
- 1 tablespoon olive oil
- 1 large onion, diced
- 2 cloves garlic, minced
- 1 carrot, diced
- 1 celery stalk, diced
- 1 can (15 ounces) diced tomatoes
- 4 cups vegetable broth
- 1 teaspoon ground cumin
- 1 teaspoon smoked paprika
- 1 teaspoon dried thyme
- Salt and pepper to taste
- 2 tablespoons fresh parsley, chopped (optional)

1. Sauté Vegetables: In a large pot, heat olive oil over medium heat.

Add onion, garlic, carrot, and celery. Sauté for about 5-7 minutes until vegetables are softened.
2. Add Lentils and Spices: Stir in lentils, cumin, smoked paprika, and dried thyme. Cook for 1-2 minutes until fragrant.
3. Add Tomatoes and Broth: Pour in the diced tomatoes and vegetable broth. Bring to a boil, then reduce heat to low and simmer for 20-25 minutes, or until lentils are tender.
4. Season and Serve: Season with salt and pepper to taste. Stir in fresh parsley if using. Serve warm.

Nutritional Information (per serving): Calories: 220 | Protein: 12g | Carbohydrates: 34g | Fats: 5g | Fiber: 14g | Cholesterol: 0mg | Sodium: 450mg

Health Benefits: This lentil and tomato stew are high in plant-based protein, fiber, and essential nutrients, making it a hearty and nutritious meal that supports weight loss and overall health.

Barley Risotto with Mushrooms

Serves:4 | Prep Time:10 min | Cook Time:20 min

- 1 cup quick-cooking barley
- 2 tablespoons olive oil
- 1 large onion, finely chopped
- 3 cloves garlic, minced
- 1 pound mushrooms, sliced (e.g., cremini, shiitake, or button)
- 1/2 cup dry white wine (optional)
- 3 cups vegetable broth, warmed
- 1/2 cup grated Parmesan cheese (optional)
- 2 tablespoons fresh parsley, chopped
- Salt and pepper to taste

1. Sauté Onions and Garlic: In a large pot or deep skillet, heat olive oil over medium heat. Add chopped onion and cook until translucent, about 3-4 minutes. Add minced garlic and cook for another 1-2 minutes until fragrant.
2. Cook Mushrooms: Add the sliced mushrooms to the pot and cook until they release their moisture and begin to brown, about 5-6 minutes.
3. Add Barley: Stir in the quick-cooking barley and cook for 1-2 minutes to lightly toast the grains.
4. Add Wine (Optional): Pour in the white wine and cook, stirring frequently, until the liquid is absorbed, about 1-2 minutes.
5. Cook Barley: Begin adding the warmed vegetable broth, one cup at a time, stirring frequently and allowing the liquid to be absorbed before adding more. Continue this process until the barley is tender and creamy, about 10-12 minutes.
6. Finish Risotto: Stir in grated Parmesan cheese (if using) and fresh parsley. Season with salt and pepper to taste.
7. Serve: Serve warm, garnished with additional parsley if desired.

Nutritional Information (per serving):
Calories: 300 | Protein: 10g | Carbohydrates: 50g | Fats: 8g | Fiber: 9g | Cholesterol: 5mg | Sodium: 400mg

Health Benefits: This quick barley risotto is a nutritious alternative to traditional risotto, providing whole grains rich in fiber and protein, combined with the umami flavor of mushrooms for a hearty and satisfying meal.

Spicy Black Bean and Quinoa Bowls

Serves:4 | Prep Time:15 min | Cook Time:20 min

- 1 cup quinoa, rinsed
- 2 cups water or vegetable broth
- 1 can (15 ounces) black beans, drained and rinsed
- 1 cup corn kernels (fresh, canned, or frozen)
- 1 red bell pepper, diced
- 1 avocado, diced
- 1/4 cup red onion, finely chopped
- 1 jalapeño, seeded and minced (optional)
- 2 tablespoons olive oil
- 1 tablespoon lime juice
- 1 teaspoon ground cumin
- 1/2 teaspoon smoked paprika
- Salt and pepper to taste
- Fresh cilantro for garnish (optional)

1. Cook Quinoa: In a medium saucepan, bring water or vegetable broth to a boil. Add quinoa, reduce heat to low, cover, and simmer for about 15 minutes until the quinoa is tender and the water is absorbed. Fluff with a fork and set aside.
2. Prepare Veggies: In a large bowl, combine black beans, corn, red bell pepper, avocado, red onion, and jalapeño (if using).
3. Make Dressing: In a small bowl, whisk together olive oil, lime juice, ground cumin, smoked paprika, salt, and pepper.
4. Combine and Toss: Add the cooked quinoa to the bowl with the vegetables. Pour the dressing over the top and toss to combine.
5. Serve: Divide the mixture among four bowls. Garnish with fresh cilantro if desired.

Nutritional Information (per serving): Calories: 300 | Protein: 10g | Carbohydrates: 40g | Fats: 12g | Fiber: 10g | Cholesterol: 0mg | Sodium: 300mg

Health Benefits: These quinoa bowls are packed with plant-based protein, fiber, and healthy fats, making them a nutritious and satisfying meal that supports weight loss and overall health.

Mediterranean Split Pea Soup

Serves:4 | Prep Time:10 min | Cook Time:20 min

- 2 cups canned or pre-cooked split peas, rinsed and drained
- 1 tablespoon olive oil
- 1 large onion, diced
- 2 carrots, diced
- 2 celery stalks, diced
- 3 cloves garlic, minced
- 1 teaspoon dried oregano
- 1 teaspoon dried thyme
- 1 bay leaf
- 4 cups vegetable broth
- 1 can (14.5 ounces) diced tomatoes
- Salt and pepper to taste
- 2 tablespoons fresh parsley, chopped (optional)

1. Sauté Vegetables: In a large pot, heat olive oil over medium heat. Add diced onion, carrots, and celery. Cook for about 5 minutes until the vegetables are softened.
2. Add Garlic and Herbs: Stir in minced garlic, dried oregano, dried thyme, and bay leaf. Cook for another 1-2 minutes until fragrant.
3. Add Split Peas and Broth: Add the rinsed and drained split peas and vegetable broth to the pot. Bring to a boil, then reduce heat to low and simmer for 10 minutes, stirring occasionally.
4. Add Tomatoes and Season: Stir in the diced tomatoes and continue to simmer for an additional 5 minutes or until the soup is heated through. Remove the bay leaf and season with salt and pepper to taste.
5. Serve: Ladle the soup into bowls and garnish with fresh parsley if desired.

Nutritional Information (per serving):
Calories: 250 | Protein: 12g | Carbohydrates: 45g | Fats: 4g | Fiber: 12g | Cholesterol: 0mg | Sodium: 600mg

Health Benefits: This quick split pea soup is rich in plant-based protein and fiber, making it a hearty and nutritious meal that supports digestive health and overall wellness. The use of fresh vegetables and herbs aligns with the Mediterranean Diet's emphasis on fresh, nutritious ingredients.

Greek-Style Rice and Beans

Serves:4 | Prep Time:10 min | Cook Time:25 min

- 1 cup long-grain rice
- 2 tablespoons olive oil
- 1 onion, finely chopped
- 3 cloves garlic, minced
- 1 can (15 ounces) cannellini beans, drained and rinsed
- 1 can (14.5 ounces) diced tomatoes
- 1 teaspoon dried oregano
- 1 teaspoon dried thyme
- 1/2 teaspoon ground cumin
- 2 cups vegetable broth
- Salt and pepper to taste
- 1/4 cup fresh parsley, chopped
- 1/4 cup crumbled feta cheese (optional)
- Lemon wedges for serving

1.Sauté Onion and Garlic: In a large pot, heat olive oil over medium heat. Add chopped onion and cook until translucent, about 5 minutes. Add minced garlic and cook for another 1-2 minutes until fragrant.
2. Add Rice and Spices: Stir in the rice, dried oregano, dried thyme, and ground cumin. Cook for 1-2 minutes to lightly toast the rice.
3. Add Tomatoes and Broth: Pour in the diced tomatoes and vegetable broth. Bring to a boil, then reduce heat to low and simmer, covered, for about 15 minutes.
4. Add Beans and Season: Stir in the cannellini beans, cover, and cook for an additional 5 minutes, or until the rice is tender and the liquid is absorbed. Season with salt and pepper to taste.
5. Serve: Stir in fresh parsley and top with crumbled feta cheese if desired. Serve with lemon wedges on the side.

Nutritional Information (per serving): Calories: 300 | Protein: 9g | Carbohydrates: 50g | Fats: 8g | Fiber: 6g | Cholesterol: 10mg | Sodium: 400mg

Health Benefits: This Greek-style rice and beans dish is a balanced meal rich in plant-based protein, fiber, and healthy fats, making it a nutritious and satisfying option for maintaining overall health.

Freekeh Salad with Pomegranate Seeds

Serves:4 | Prep Time:15 min | Cook Time:20 min

- 1 cup freekeh
- 2 cups water or vegetable broth
- 1/2 cup pomegranate seeds
- 1/2 cup chopped cucumber
- 1/2 cup chopped bell pepper
- 1/4 cup chopped red onion
- 1/4 cup chopped fresh parsley
- 1/4 cup chopped fresh mint
- 3 tablespoons olive oil
- 2 tablespoons lemon juice
- 1 tablespoon balsamic vinegar
- Salt and pepper to taste

1. Cook Freekeh: In a medium saucepan, bring water or vegetable broth to a boil. Add freekeh, reduce heat to low, cover, and simmer for about 20 minutes until tender. Drain any excess liquid and let it cool.
2. Prepare Vegetables: In a large bowl, combine pomegranate seeds, cucumber, bell pepper, red onion, parsley, and mint.

3. Make Dressing: In a small bowl, whisk together olive oil, lemon juice, balsamic vinegar, salt, and pepper.

4. Combine Salad: Add the cooled freekeh to the bowl with the vegetables. Pour the dressing over the top and toss gently to combine.

5. Serve: Serve the salad chilled or at room temperature.

Nutritional Information (per serving): Calories: 250 | Protein: 6g | Carbohydrates: 35g | Fats: 10g | Fiber: 8g | Cholesterol: 0mg | Sodium: 150mg

Health Benefits: This freekeh salad is packed with fiber, antioxidants, and vitamins from whole grains and fresh vegetables, making it a nutritious and flavorful option that supports weight loss and overall health.

Chickpea and Spinach Stew

Serves:4 | Prep Time:10 min | Cook Time:30 min

- 2 tablespoons olive oil
- 1 large onion, diced
- 3 cloves garlic, minced
- 1 teaspoon ground cumin
- 1 teaspoon smoked paprika
- 1/2 teaspoon ground coriander
- 1/2 teaspoon ground turmeric
- 1 can (15 ounces) diced tomatoes
- 4 cups vegetable broth
- 2 cans (15 ounces each) chickpeas, drained and rinsed
- 4 cups fresh spinach, chopped
- Salt and pepper to taste
- 1/4 cup fresh cilantro, chopped (optional)
- Lemon wedges for serving

1. Sauté Onion and Garlic: In a large pot, heat olive oil over medium heat. Add diced onion and cook until translucent, about 5 minutes. Add minced garlic and cook for another 1-2 minutes until fragrant.

2. Add Spices: Stir in ground cumin, smoked paprika, ground coriander, and ground turmeric. Cook for 1-2 minutes to toast the spices.

3. Add Tomatoes and Broth: Pour in the diced tomatoes and vegetable broth. Bring to a boil, then reduce heat to low and simmer for 10 minutes.

4. Add Chickpeas and Spinach: Stir in the chickpeas and chopped spinach. Simmer for another 10-15 minutes, or until the spinach is wilted and the stew is heated through. Season with salt and pepper to taste.

5. Serve: Ladle the stew into bowls, garnish with fresh cilantro if desired, and serve with lemon wedges on the side.

Nutritional Information (per serving): Calories: 250 | Protein: 10g | Carbohydrates: 35g | Fats: 8g | Fiber: 10g | Cholesterol: 0mg | Sodium: 500mg

30

Health Benefits: This chickpea and spinach stew is rich in plant-based protein, fiber, and essential vitamins, making it a hearty and nutritious meal that supports digestive health and overall wellness.

Wild Rice Pilaf with Herbs

Serves:4 | Prep Time:10 min | Cook Time:20 min

- 1 cup quick-cooking wild rice or wild rice blend
- 2 cups vegetable broth
- 2 tablespoons olive oil
- 1 large onion, finely chopped
- 2 cloves garlic, minced
- 1 carrot, diced
- 1 celery stalk, diced
- 1/4 cup dried cranberries
- 1/4 cup chopped fresh parsley
- 2 tablespoons chopped fresh dill
- 1 tablespoon chopped fresh thyme
- Salt and pepper to taste
- 1/4 cup chopped walnuts or pecans (optional)

1. Cook Wild Rice: In a medium saucepan, bring vegetable broth to a boil. Add quick-cooking wild rice, reduce heat to low, cover, and simmer for about 15 minutes, or until the rice is tender and the liquid is absorbed. Fluff with a fork and set aside.

2. Sauté Vegetables: In a large skillet, heat olive oil over medium heat. Add chopped onion and cook until translucent, about 3-4 minutes. Add minced garlic, diced carrot, and diced celery. Cook for another 5 minutes until the vegetables are tender.

3. Combine Ingredients: Stir in the cooked wild rice, dried cranberries, fresh parsley, dill, and thyme. Cook for another 2-3 minutes until heated through. Season with salt and pepper to taste.

4. Add Nuts (Optional): Stir in chopped walnuts or pecans if using.

5. Serve: Transfer the pilaf to a serving dish and serve warm.

Nutritional Information (per serving): Calories: 250 | Protein: 6g | Carbohydrates: 40g | Fats: 8g | Fiber: 5g | Cholesterol: 0mg | Sodium: 400mg

Health Benefits: This quick wild rice pilaf is packed with fiber, vitamins, and antioxidants from wild rice and fresh herbs, making it a nutritious and flavorful dish that supports overall health and well-being. The combination of vegetables, dried cranberries, and nuts provides essential nutrients, aligning with the Mediterranean Diet's emphasis on fresh, nutritious ingredients.

Lentil and Carrot Soup

Serves:4 | Prep Time:10 min | Cook Time:35 min

- 2 tablespoons olive oil
- 1 large onion, chopped
- 3 cloves garlic, minced
- 2 carrots, diced
- 1 cup dried lentils, rinsed
- 1 teaspoon ground cumin
- 1/2 teaspoon ground coriander
- 1/2 teaspoon smoked paprika
- 1/4 teaspoon turmeric
- 6 cups vegetable broth
- 1 can (14.5 ounces) diced tomatoes
- Salt and pepper to taste
- 2 tablespoons fresh parsley, chopped (optional)

1. Sauté Vegetables: In a large pot, heat olive oil over medium heat. Add chopped onion and cook until translucent, about 5 minutes. Add minced garlic and cook for another 1-2 minutes until fragrant.
2. Add Carrots and Spices: Stir in diced carrots, ground cumin, ground coriander, smoked paprika, and turmeric. Cook for 1-2 minutes to toast the spices.
3. Add Lentils and Broth: Add the rinsed lentils and vegetable broth. Bring to a boil, then reduce heat to low and simmer for 20 minutes.
4. Add Tomatoes: Stir in the diced tomatoes and continue to simmer for another 10-15 minutes, or until the lentils and carrots are tender. Season with salt and pepper to taste.
5. Serve: Ladle the soup into bowls, garnish with fresh parsley if desired, and serve warm.

Nutritional Information (per serving): Calories: 220 | Protein: 10g | Carbohydrates: 32g | Fats: 7g | Fiber: 12g | Cholesterol: 0mg | Sodium: 500mg

Health Benefits: This lentil and carrot soup is rich in plant-based protein, fiber, and essential vitamins, making it a hearty and nutritious meal that supports digestive health and overall wellness.

Bulgur Wheat Salad with Mint

Serves:4 | Prep Time:15 min | Cook Time:10 min

- 1 cup bulgur wheat
- 2 cups water
- 1/2 cup fresh mint leaves, chopped
- 1/2 cup fresh parsley, chopped
- 1/2 cup cherry tomatoes, halved
- 1/2 cucumber, diced
- 1/4 cup red onion, finely chopped
- 1/4 cup fresh lemon juice
- 3 tablespoons olive oil
- Salt and pepper to taste

1. Cook Bulgur: In a medium saucepan, bring water to a boil. Stir in bulgur wheat, cover, and remove from heat. Let it sit for about 10 minutes, or until the bulgur is tender and has absorbed the water. Fluff with a fork and let it cool.
2. Prepare Vegetables: In a large bowl, combine chopped mint, parsley, cherry tomatoes, cucumber, and red onion.
3. Make Dressing: In a small bowl, whisk together lemon juice, olive oil, salt, and pepper.
4. Combine Salad: Add the cooked bulgur to the bowl with the vegetables. Pour the dressing over the top and toss gently to combine.
5. Serve: Serve the salad chilled or at room temperature.

Nutritional Information (per serving): Calories: 180 | Protein: 4g | Carbohydrates: 24g | Fats: 8g | Fiber: 6g | Cholesterol: 0mg | Sodium: 150mg

Health Benefits: This bulgur wheat salad is rich in fiber, vitamins, and antioxidants from the fresh herbs and vegetables, making it a nutritious and refreshing dish that supports digestive health and overall wellness.

White Bean and Kale Soup

Serves:4 | Prep Time:10 min | Cook Time:30 min

- 2 tablespoons olive oil
- 1 large onion, chopped
- 3 cloves garlic, minced
- 2 carrots, diced
- 2 celery stalks, diced
- 1 can (15 ounces) cannellini beans, drained and rinsed
- 4 cups vegetable broth
- 2 cups chopped kale
- 1 teaspoon dried thyme
- 1 teaspoon dried rosemary
- 1 bay leaf
- Salt and pepper to taste
- 1 tablespoon lemon juice
- Fresh parsley for garnish (optional)

1. Sauté Vegetables: In a large pot, heat olive oil over medium heat. Add chopped onion, carrots, and celery. Cook for about 5-7 minutes until the vegetables are softened. Add minced garlic and cook for another 1-2 minutes until fragrant.
2. Add Beans and Broth: Stir in the cannellini beans, vegetable broth, dried thyme, dried rosemary, and bay leaf. Bring to a boil, then reduce heat to low and simmer for 20 minutes.
3. Add Kale: Stir in the chopped kale and continue to simmer for another 10 minutes, or until the kale is tender.
4. Season and Serve: Remove the bay leaf and stir in the lemon juice. Season with salt and pepper to taste. Ladle the soup into bowls and garnish with fresh parsley if desired.

Nutritional Information (per serving): Calories: 220 | Protein: 7g | Carbohydrates: 28g | Fats: 8g Fiber: 7g | Cholesterol: 0mg | Sodium: 500mg

Health Benefits: This white bean and kale soup is packed with plant-based protein, fiber, and essential vitamins, making it a hearty and nutritious meal that supports digestive health and overall wellness.

Quinoa Stuffed Bell Peppers

Serves:4 | Prep Time:15 min | Cook Time:30 min

- 4 large bell peppers (any color)
- 1 cup quinoa, rinsed
- 2 cups vegetable broth or water
- 1 tablespoon olive oil
- 1 small onion, chopped
- 2 cloves garlic, minced
- 1 cup cherry tomatoes, halved
- 1 cup black beans, drained and rinsed
- 1/2 cup corn kernels (fresh or frozen)
- 1 teaspoon ground cumin
- 1 teaspoon smoked paprika
- Salt and pepper to taste
- 1/4 cup fresh cilantro, chopped
- 1/2 cup shredded cheese (optional)

1. Preheat Oven: Preheat your oven to 375°F (190°C).
2. Cook Quinoa: In a medium saucepan, bring vegetable broth or water to a boil. Add quinoa, reduce heat to low, cover, and simmer for about 15 minutes until the quinoa is tender and the liquid is absorbed. Fluff with a fork and set aside.
3. Prepare Bell Peppers: Cut the tops off the bell peppers and remove the seeds. Place them in a baking dish.
4. Sauté Vegetables: In a large skillet, heat olive oil over medium heat. Add chopped onion and cook until translucent, about 5 minutes. Add minced garlic and cook for another 1-2 minutes until fragrant.
5. Combine Filling: Stir in the cooked quinoa, cherry tomatoes, black beans, corn, ground cumin, smoked paprika, salt, and pepper. Cook for 3-5 minutes until heated through. Remove from heat and stir in fresh cilantro.
6. Stuff Peppers: Spoon the quinoa mixture into each bell pepper, filling them to the top. If using, sprinkle shredded cheese on top of each pepper.
7. Bake: Cover the baking dish with foil and bake in the preheated oven for 25 minutes. Remove the foil and bake for an additional 5 minutes, or until the peppers are tender and the cheese is melted and golden.
8. Serve: Serve warm, garnished with additional fresh cilantro if desired.

Nutritional Information (per serving): Calories: 300 | Protein: 10g | Carbohydrates: 45g | Fats: 8g | Fiber: 10g | Cholesterol: 10mg | Sodium: 400mg

Health Benefits: These quinoa stuffed bell peppers are packed with plant-based protein, fibre, and essential nutrients, making them a nutritious and satisfying meal that supports weight loss and overall health.

Mediterranean Black-Eyed Peas

Serves:4 | Prep Time:10 min | Cook Time:30 min

- 2 tablespoons olive oil
- 1 large onion, chopped
- 3 cloves garlic, minced
- 1 red bell pepper, diced
- 1 can (15 ounces) black-eyed peas, drained and rinsed
- 1 can (14.5 ounces) diced tomatoes
- 1 cup vegetable broth
- 1 teaspoon dried oregano
- 1 teaspoon dried thyme
- 1/2 teaspoon smoked paprika
- Salt and pepper to taste
- 2 tablespoons fresh parsley, chopped
- Lemon wedges for serving

1. Sauté Vegetables: Heat olive oil over medium heat in a large pot. Add chopped onion and cook until translucent, about 5 minutes. Add minced garlic and diced red bell pepper, cooking for another 5 minutes until softened.
2. Add Black-Eyed Peas and Tomatoes: Stir in the black-eyed peas, diced tomatoes, vegetable broth, dried oregano, dried thyme, and smoked paprika. Bring to a boil, then reduce heat to low and simmer for about 20 minutes, or until the flavors meld and the mixture thickens slightly.
3. Season and Serve: Season with salt and pepper to taste. Stir in fresh parsley. Serve warm with lemon wedges on the side.

Nutritional Information (per serving): Calories: 220 | Protein: 7g | Carbohydrates: 28g | Fats: 8g | Fiber: 8g | Cholesterol: 0mg | Sodium: 400mg

Health Benefits: This dish is rich in plant-based protein, fiber, and essential vitamins, making it a hearty and nutritious meal that supports digestive health and overall wellness.

CHAPTER 4

POULTRY – LEAN AND FLAVORFUL CHICKEN AND TURKEY DISHES

Lemon Herb Grilled Chicken

Serves:4 | Prep Time:15 min | Cook Time:20 min

- 4 boneless, skinless chicken breasts
- 1/4 cup olive oil
- Zest and juice of 1 lemon
- 3 cloves garlic, minced
- 1 tablespoon fresh rosemary, chopped
- 1 tablespoon fresh thyme, chopped
- 1 teaspoon dried oregano
- Salt and pepper to taste
- Lemon wedges for serving

1. Prepare Marinade: In a bowl, whisk together olive oil, lemon zest, lemon juice, minced garlic, rosemary, thyme, oregano, salt, and pepper.
2. Marinate Chicken: Place the chicken breasts in a resealable plastic bag or a shallow dish. Pour the marinade over the chicken, ensuring all pieces are well coated. Marinate in the refrigerator for at least 30 minutes, preferably 1-2 hours.
3. Preheat Grill: Preheat your grill to medium-high heat.
4. Grill Chicken: Remove the chicken from the marinade and discard any remaining marinade. Grill the chicken for 6-8 minutes per side, or until fully cooked and the internal temperature reaches 165°F (75°C).
5. Serve: Serve the grilled chicken with lemon wedges on the side.

Nutritional Information (per serving): Calories: 250 | Protein: 30g | Carbohydrates: 1g | Fats: 14g | Fiber: 0g | Cholesterol: 70mg | Sodium: 150mg

Health Benefits: This lemon herb grilled chicken is a lean and flavorful protein option, providing essential nutrients and healthy fats from olive oil and fresh herbs, supporting weight loss and overall health.

Greek Chicken Souvlaki

Serves:4 | Prep Time:20 min | Cook Time:15 min

- 1 1/2 pounds boneless, skinless chicken breasts, cut into 1-inch pieces
- 1/4 cup olive oil
- Juice of 1 lemon
- 3 cloves garlic, minced
- 1 tablespoon dried oregano
- 1 teaspoon dried thyme
- Salt and pepper to taste
- Wooden skewers, soaked in water for 30 minutes

1. Prepare Marinade: In a bowl, whisk together olive oil, lemon juice, minced garlic, dried oregano, dried thyme, salt, and pepper.
2. Marinate Chicken: Place the chicken pieces in a resealable plastic bag or a shallow dish. Pour the marinade over the chicken, ensuring all pieces are well coated. Marinate in the refrigerator for at least 30 minutes, preferably 1-2 hours.
3. Preheat Grill: Preheat your grill to medium-high heat.
4. Skewer Chicken: Thread the marinated chicken pieces onto the soaked wooden skewers.
5. Grill Chicken: Grill the chicken skewers for 10-15 minutes, turning occasionally, until fully cooked and the internal temperature reaches 165°F (75°C).
6. Serve: Serve the chicken souvlaki with your favorite sides such as tzatziki, pita bread, and a Greek salad.

Nutritional Information (per serving): Calories: 280 | Protein: 30g | Carbohydrates: 1g | Fats: 18g | Fiber: 0g | Cholesterol: 70mg | Sodium: 200mg

Health Benefits: Greek chicken souvlaki is a lean and flavorful protein option, providing essential nutrients and healthy fats from olive oil and herbs, supporting weight loss and overall health.

Mediterranean Chicken Stew

Serves:4 | Prep Time:10 min | Cook Time:20 min

- 2 tablespoons olive oil
- 1 large onion, chopped
- 3 cloves garlic, minced
- 1 pound boneless, skinless chicken thighs, cut into small bite-sized pieces
- 1 red bell pepper, diced
- 1 zucchini, diced
- 1 can (14.5 ounces) diced tomatoes

- 1 cup chicken broth
- 1/2 cup Kalamata olives, pitted and sliced
- 1 teaspoon dried oregano
- 1 teaspoon dried thyme
- 1/2 teaspoon smoked paprika
- Salt and pepper to taste
- 2 tablespoons fresh parsley, chopped (optional)
- Lemon wedges for serving

1. Sauté Onion and Garlic: In a large pot, heat olive oil over medium-high heat. Add chopped onion and cook until translucent, about 3 minutes. Add minced garlic and cook for another 1 minute until fragrant.

2. Brown Chicken: Add the chicken pieces to the pot and cook, stirring occasionally, until browned on all sides, about 5 minutes.

3. Add Vegetables and Spices: Stir in the red bell pepper, zucchini, diced tomatoes, chicken broth, Kalamata olives, dried oregano, dried thyme, smoked paprika, salt, and pepper. Bring to a boil, then reduce heat to medium and simmer for 10 minutes, or until the chicken is cooked through and the vegetables are tender.

4. Finish and Serve: Stir in fresh parsley if using. Serve the stew warm with lemon wedges on the side.

Nutritional Information (per serving): Calories: 300 | Protein: 22g | Carbohydrates: 12g | Fats: 18g | Fiber: 4g | Cholesterol: 70mg | Sodium: 600mg

Health Benefits: This quick Mediterranean chicken stew is rich in protein, healthy fats, and essential nutrients, making it a hearty and nutritious meal that supports overall health and wellness. The combination of chicken, vegetables, and olives provides a balanced and flavorful dish that aligns with the Mediterranean Diet's emphasis on fresh, nutritious ingredients.

Balsamic Glazed Turkey Meatballs

Serves:4 | Prep Time:15 min | Cook Time:25 min

- 1 pound ground turkey
- 1/4 cup breadcrumbs
- 1/4 cup grated Parmesan cheese
- 1 egg, beaten
- 2 cloves garlic, minced
- 1 tablespoon fresh parsley, chopped
- 1 teaspoon dried oregano
- Salt and pepper to taste
- 2 tablespoons olive oil
- 1/2 cup balsamic vinegar
- 2 tablespoons honey
- 1 tablespoon soy sauce

1. Preheat Oven: Preheat your oven to 375°F (190°C). Line a baking sheet with parchment paper or lightly grease it.

2. Mix Meatball Ingredients: In a large bowl, combine ground turkey, breadcrumbs, Parmesan cheese, beaten egg, minced garlic, chopped parsley, dried oregano, salt, and pepper. Mix until well combined.

3. Form Meatballs: Shape the mixture into small meatballs, about 1 inch in diameter, and place them on the prepared baking sheet.

4. Bake Meatballs: Bake in the preheated oven for 15-20 minutes, or until cooked through and golden brown.

5. Prepare Glaze: While the meatballs are baking, heat olive oil in a small saucepan over medium heat. Add balsamic vinegar, honey, and soy sauce. Bring to a simmer and cook for about 5 minutes, or until the glaze is thickened.

6. Glaze Meatballs: Once the meatballs are done baking, transfer them to a large bowl. Pour the balsamic glaze over the meatballs and toss to coat evenly.

7. Serve: Serve the meatballs warm, garnished with additional fresh parsley if desired.

Nutritional Information (per serving): Calories: 300 | Protein: 25g | Carbohydrates: 15g | Fats: 15g | Fiber: 1g | Cholesterol: 95mg | Sodium: 450mg

Health Benefits: These balsamic glazed turkey meatballs are a lean source of protein, combined with the rich flavors of balsamic vinegar and honey, making them a nutritious and delicious option for any meal.

Garlic and Herb Roasted Chicken

Serves:4 | Prep Time:10 min | Cook Time:20 min

- 4 chicken pieces (thighs, drumsticks, or breasts)
- 4 tablespoons olive oil
- 4 cloves garlic, minced
- 1 tablespoon fresh rosemary, chopped
- 1 tablespoon fresh thyme, chopped
- 1 tablespoon fresh parsley, chopped
- 1 lemon, cut into wedges
- Salt and pepper to taste

1. Preheat Oven: Preheat your oven to 425°F (220°C).

2. Prepare Chicken: Pat the chicken pieces dry with paper towels. In a small bowl, mix together olive oil, minced garlic, rosemary, thyme, parsley, salt, and pepper.

3. Season Chicken: Rub the garlic and herb mixture all over the chicken pieces. Place lemon wedges in the roasting pan or on the baking sheet.

4. Roast Chicken: Place the chicken pieces on a baking sheet or in a roasting pan. Roast in the preheated oven for about 20-25 minutes, or until the internal temperature reaches 165°F (75°C) and the juices run clear when the thickest part is pierced.

5. Rest and Serve: Let the chicken rest for 5 min

before serving. Serve with your favorite sides.

Nutritional Information (per serving):
Calories: 350 | Protein: 28g | Carbohydrates: 1g | Fats: 25g | Fiber: 0g | Cholesterol: 110mg | Sodium: 300mg

Health Benefits: This garlic and herb roasted chicken is a lean source of protein, combined with healthy fats from olive oil. The herbs provide antioxidants and anti-inflammatory benefits, making this dish a nutritious and flavorful option for a balanced meal.

Chicken and Artichoke Skillet

Serves:4 | Prep Time:10 min | Cook Time:25 min

- 2 tablespoons olive oil
- 1 pound boneless, skinless chicken thighs, cut into bite-sized pieces
- 1 large onion, chopped
- 3 cloves garlic, minced
- 1 can (14 ounces) artichoke hearts, drained and quartered
- 1 cup cherry tomatoes, halved
- 1/2 cup chicken broth
- 1/4 cup dry white wine (optional)
- 1 teaspoon dried oregano
- 1 teaspoon dried thyme
- Salt and pepper to taste
- 2 tablespoons fresh parsley, chopped
- Lemon wedges for serving

1. Heat Oil: In a large skillet, heat olive oil over medium-high heat.
2. Cook Chicken: Add the chicken pieces to the skillet, season with salt and pepper, and cook until browned and cooked through, about 5-7 minutes. Remove the chicken from the skillet and set aside.
3. Sauté Vegetables: In the same skillet, add the chopped onion and cook until softened, about 5 minutes. Add minced garlic and cook for another 1-2 minutes until fragrant.
4. Add Artichokes and Tomatoes: Stir in the artichoke hearts and cherry tomatoes. Cook for about 3-4 minutes until the tomatoes begin to soften.
5. Deglaze Pan: Pour in the chicken broth and white wine (if using). Stir in dried oregano and thyme. Bring to a simmer.
6. Combine and Simmer: Return the chicken to the skillet. Simmer for about 5-7 minutes until the flavors meld and the sauce thickens slightly.
7. Serve: Garnish with fresh parsley and serve with lemon wedges on the side.

Nutritional Information (per serving): Calories: 280 | Protein: 22g | Carbohydrates: 10g | Fats: 16g | Fiber: 4g | Cholesterol: 70mg | Sodium: 350mg

Health Benefits: This chicken and artichoke

skillet is a nutritious and flavorful dish, rich in protein and fiber, with the health benefits of artichokes and tomatoes, supporting overall health and wellness.

Turkey and Zucchini Meatballs

Serves:4 | Prep Time:15 min | Cook Time:20 min

- 1 pound ground turkey
- 1 medium zucchini, grated
- 1/4 cup breadcrumbs
- 1/4 cup grated Parmesan cheese
- 1 egg, beaten
- 2 cloves garlic, minced
- 1 tablespoon fresh parsley, chopped
- 1 teaspoon dried oregano
- Salt and pepper to taste
- 2 tablespoons olive oil

1. Preheat Oven: Preheat your oven to 375°F (190°C). Line a baking sheet with parchment paper.
2. Prepare Meatball Mixture: In a large bowl, combine ground turkey, grated zucchini, breadcrumbs, Parmesan cheese, beaten egg, minced garlic, parsley, oregano, salt, and pepper. Mix until well combined.
3. Form Meatballs: Shape the mixture into small meatballs, about 1 inch in diameter, and place them on the prepared baking sheet.
4. Bake Meatballs: Bake in the preheated oven for 15-20 minutes, or until cooked through and golden brown.
5. Serve: Serve the meatballs warm, garnished with additional fresh parsley if desired.

Nutritional Information (per serving): Calories: 250 | Protein: 25g | Carbohydrates: 6g | Fats: 14g | Fiber: 1g | Cholesterol: 95mg | Sodium: 300mg

Health Benefits: These turkey and zucchini meatballs are a lean source of protein, combined with the fiber and nutrients from zucchini, making them a nutritious and delicious option for any meal.

Lemon Dill Chicken Salad

Serves:4 | Prep Time:15 min | Cook Time:20 min

- 2 boneless, skinless chicken breasts
- 1/4 cup olive oil
- Juice and zest of 1 lemon
- 2 tablespoons fresh dill, chopped
- 1/2 cup Greek yogurt
- 1/4 cup mayonnaise
- 2 celery stalks, finely chopped
- 1/4 cup red onion, finely chopped
- Salt and pepper to taste
- Mixed greens for serving (optional)

1. Cook Chicken: Preheat oven to 375°F (190°C). Place chicken breasts on a baking

sheet, drizzle with olive oil, and season with salt and pepper. Bake for 20 minutes, or until fully cooked. Let cool and then dice into bite-sized pieces.

2. Prepare Dressing: In a large bowl, combine Greek yogurt, mayonnaise, lemon juice, lemon zest, and chopped dill. Mix until well combined.

3. Combine Salad: Add the diced chicken, celery, and red onion to the bowl with the dressing. Stir until the chicken is evenly coated with the dressing. Season with salt and pepper to taste.

4. Serve: Serve the chicken salad on a bed of mixed greens or in sandwiches.

Nutritional Information (per serving): Calories: 280 | Protein: 25g | Carbohydrates: 4g | Fats: 18g | Fiber: 1g | Cholesterol: 70mg | Sodium: 250mg

Health Benefits: This lemon dill chicken salad is a lean and flavorful protein option, combined with the health benefits of Greek yogurt and fresh herbs, making it a nutritious and delicious meal for any occasion.

Greek Chicken Gyro Wraps

Serves:4 | Prep Time:15 min | Cook Time:20 min

- 2 boneless, skinless chicken breasts
- 1/4 cup olive oil
- Juice of 1 lemon
- 3 cloves garlic, minced
- 1 tablespoon dried oregano
- Salt and pepper to taste
- 4 pita breads or flatbreads
- 1 cup tzatziki sauce
- 1/2 cup cherry tomatoes, halved
- 1/2 cucumber, thinly sliced
- 1/4 red onion, thinly sliced
- Fresh lettuce leaves

1. Marinate Chicken: In a bowl, combine olive oil, lemon juice, minced garlic, dried oregano, salt, and pepper. Add the chicken breasts and marinate in the refrigerator for at least 30 minutes, preferably 1-2 hours.

2. Cook Chicken: Preheat grill or skillet over medium-high heat. Grill or cook the chicken breasts for about 6-8 minutes per side, or until fully cooked and the internal temperature reaches 165°F (75°C). Let rest for a few minutes, then slice into strips.

3. Prepare Wraps: Warm the pita breads or flatbreads in a skillet or oven. Spread a generous amount of tzatziki sauce on each pita.

4. Assemble Gyros: Top with sliced chicken, cherry tomatoes, cucumber, red onion, and lettuce leaves.

5. Serve: Wrap the pitas and serve immediately.

Nutritional Information (per serving): Calories: 400 | Protein: 30g | Carbohydrates: 30g |

Fats: 18g | Fiber: 3g | Cholesterol: 70mg | Sodium: 400mg

Health Benefits: These Greek chicken gyro wraps are a balanced meal, providing lean protein from the chicken, healthy fats from olive oil, and vitamins from fresh vegetables, making them a nutritious and satisfying option.

Spicy Harissa Chicken

Serves:4 | Prep Time:15 min | Cook Time:25 min

- 4 boneless, skinless chicken breasts
- 3 tablespoons harissa paste
- 2 tablespoons olive oil
- Juice of 1 lemon
- 3 cloves garlic, minced
- 1 teaspoon ground cumin
- Salt and pepper to taste
- Fresh cilantro or parsley for garnish (optional)

1. Preheat Oven: Preheat your oven to 375°F (190°C).

2. Prepare Marinade: In a bowl, combine harissa paste, olive oil, lemon juice, minced garlic, ground cumin, salt, and pepper.

3. Marinate Chicken: Place the chicken breasts in a resealable plastic bag or a shallow dish. Pour the harissa marinade over the chicken, ensuring all pieces are well coated. Marinate in the refrigerator for at least 30 minutes, preferably 1-2 hours.

4. Bake Chicken: Place the marinated chicken breasts on a baking sheet lined with parchment paper. Bake in the preheated oven for 25-30 minutes, or until the chicken is fully cooked and the internal temperature reaches 165°F (75°C).

5. Serve: Garnish with fresh cilantro or parsley if desired and serve warm.

Nutritional Information (per serving): Calories: 280 | Protein: 30g | Carbohydrates: 3g | Fats: 16g | Fiber: 1g | Cholesterol: 70mg | Sodium: 400mg

Health Benefits: Spicy harissa chicken is a flavorful and lean protein option, providing the benefits of healthy fats from olive oil and the metabolism-boosting properties of spicy harissa, supporting weight loss and overall health.

Roasted Lemon Herb Turkey Breast

Serves:4 | Prep Time:10 min | Cook Time:15 min

- 4 turkey breast cutlets (about 1-1.5 pounds total)
- 1/4 cup olive oil
- Zest and juice of 1 lemon
- 4 cloves garlic, minced
- 2 tablespoons fresh rosemary, chopped
- 2 tablespoons fresh thyme, chopped

- 1 tablespoon fresh sage, chopped
- Salt and pepper to taste

1. Preheat Oven: Preheat your oven to 400°F (200°C).
2. Prepare Herb Mixture: In a small bowl, combine olive oil, lemon zest, lemon juice, minced garlic, rosemary, thyme, sage, salt, and pepper.
3. Season Turkey Cutlets: Place the turkey cutlets on a baking sheet lined with parchment paper. Rub the herb mixture all over the turkey cutlets, ensuring they are well coated on both sides.
4. Roast Turkey: Roast the turkey cutlets in the preheated oven for about 12-15 minutes, or until the internal temperature reaches 165°F (75°C) and the juices run clear.
5. Rest and Serve: Remove the turkey from the oven and let it rest for 5 minutes before serving. Serve with your favorite sides.

Nutritional Information (per serving): Calories: 350 | Protein: 45g | Carbohydrates: 1g | Fats: 18g | Fiber: 0g | Cholesterol: 120mg | Sodium: 300mg

Health Benefits: This quick lemon herb turkey breast is a lean and flavorful protein option, rich in vitamins and antioxidants from fresh herbs. The use of olive oil and fresh herbs provides healthy fats and nutrients, making it a nutritious and delicious meal for any occasion.

Chicken and Olive Tagine

Serves:4 | Prep Time:10 min | Cook Time:20 min

- 2 tablespoons olive oil
- 1 large onion, finely chopped
- 3 cloves garlic, minced
- 1 teaspoon ground cumin
- 1 teaspoon ground ginger
- 1 teaspoon ground cinnamon
- 1 teaspoon ground turmeric
- 1/2 teaspoon ground black pepper
- 1/2 teaspoon paprika
- 1/2 teaspoon ground coriander
- 4 boneless, skinless chicken thighs, cut into bite-sized pieces
- 1 cup chicken broth
- 1/2 cup green olives, pitted and halved
- 1 preserved lemon, rinsed and chopped
- 1/4 cup fresh cilantro, chopped
- 1/4 cup fresh parsley, chopped
- Salt to taste

1. Sauté Onions and Garlic: In a large skillet or tagine, heat olive oil over medium-high heat. Add chopped onion and cook until softened, about 3 minutes. Add minced garlic and cook for another 1 minute until fragrant.
2. Add Spices: Stir in ground cumin, ginger, cinnamon, turmeric, black pepper, paprika, and coriander.

Cook for 1-2 minutes until the spices are aromatic.
3. Add Chicken: Add the chicken pieces to the skillet and cook, stirring occasionally, until browned on all sides, about 5 minutes.
4. Add Broth and Simmer: Pour in the chicken broth and bring to a simmer. Reduce heat to medium and simmer for 10 minutes, or until the chicken is cooked through and tender.
5. Add Olives and Lemon: Stir in the green olives and preserved lemon. Continue to simmer for another 3-5 minutes.
6. Serve: Garnish with fresh cilantro and parsley. Serve warm with couscous or rice.

Nutritional Information (per serving): Calories: 350 | Protein: 22g | Carbohydrates: 8g | Fats: 24g | Fiber: 3g | Cholesterol: 90mg | Sodium: 600mg

Health Benefits: This quick chicken and olive tagine is a flavorful and nutritious dish, rich in protein, healthy fats, and a variety of antioxidants from spices and herbs, supporting overall health and wellness. The combination of fresh herbs and preserved lemon adds a vibrant flavor, making it a delightful meal.

Honey Balsamic Glazed Chicken Thighs

Serves:4 | Prep Time:10 min | Cook Time:20 min

- 4 boneless, skinless chicken thighs (about 1.5 lbs or 680g)
- Salt and pepper, to taste
- 2 tablespoons olive oil
- 3 tablespoons balsamic vinegar
- 2 tablespoons honey
- 2 cloves garlic, minced
- 1 teaspoon dried thyme (or 1 tablespoon fresh thyme leaves)

1. Preheat and Prepare: Preheat your oven to 400°F (200°C). Season the chicken thighs with salt and pepper on both sides.
2. Sear the Chicken: In a large oven-proof skillet, heat olive oil over medium-high heat. Add the chicken thighs and sear for 3-4 minutes on each side until golden brown. Remove chicken from skillet and set aside.
3. Make the Glaze: In the same skillet, reduce the heat to medium. Add minced garlic and cook for 1 minute until fragrant. Add balsamic vinegar, honey, and thyme to the skillet. Stir and let it simmer for 2-3 minutes until the glaze thickens slightly.
4. Glaze and Bake: Return the chicken thighs to the skillet, spooning the glaze over each piece. Transfer the skillet to the preheated oven and bake for 12-15 minutes or until the chicken is fully cooked through (internal temperature of 165°F or 74°C).
5. Serve: Remove from oven and let the chicken rest for a few minutes. Serve warm.

Nutrition Information (per serving): Calories: 320 kcal | Protein: 25g | Carbohydrates: 14g | Fat: 18g | Fiber: 0.5g | Cholesterol: 110mg | Sodium: 220mg

Health Benefits: This dish provides lean protein, heart-healthy fats from olive oil, antioxidants from balsamic vinegar, and antibacterial properties from honey.

Mediterranean Chicken and Rice

Serves:4 | Prep Time:10 min | Cook Time:20 min

- 4 boneless, skinless chicken breasts
- Salt and pepper, to taste
- 2 tablespoons olive oil
- 1 onion, finely chopped
- 3 cloves garlic, minced
- 1 red bell pepper, diced
- 1 cup cherry tomatoes, halved
- 1 teaspoon dried oregano
- 1 teaspoon dried basil
- 1/2 teaspoon smoked paprika
- 1 cup long-grain white rice
- 2 cups chicken broth
- Juice of 1 lemon
- 1/4 cup chopped fresh parsley
- Optional: Crumbled feta cheese for serving

1. Season Chicken: Season chicken breasts with salt and pepper on both sides.
2. Cook Chicken: In a large skillet, heat olive oil over medium-high heat. Add chicken breasts and cook for 4-5 minutes on each side until golden brown and cooked through. Remove chicken from skillet and set aside.
3. Saute Vegetables: In the same skillet, add chopped onion and garlic. Saute for 2-3 minutes until onion is translucent. Add diced red bell pepper and cherry tomatoes. Cook for another 2-3 minutes until vegetables are slightly softened.
4. Add Rice and Spices: Stir in dried oregano, dried basil, and smoked paprika. Add rice to the skillet, stirring to coat the rice with the flavors from the vegetables and spices.
5. Simmer with Broth: Pour in chicken broth and lemon juice. Bring to a boil, then reduce heat to low. Cover and simmer for 15-20 minutes, or until rice is tender and liquid is absorbed.
6. Combine Chicken and Rice: Slice or shred the cooked chicken breasts. Add them back to the skillet with the rice mixture, stirring gently to combine.
7. Serve: Garnish with chopped fresh parsley and crumbled feta cheese if desired. Serve hot.

Nutrition Information (per serving): Calories: 380 kcal | Protein: 30g | Carbohydrates: 42g | Fat: 10g | Fiber: 3g | Cholesterol: 80mg | Sodium: 520mg

Health Benefits: This dish provides lean protein from chicken, fiber from vegetables and rice,

antioxidants from tomatoes and herbs, and heart-healthy fats from olive oil and optional feta cheese, supporting overall health in line with the Mediterranean Diet.

Turkey Stuffed Bell Peppers

Serves:4 | Prep Time:15 min | Cook Time:30 min

- 4 large bell peppers (any color), tops cut off and seeds removed
- 1 tablespoon olive oil
- 1 onion, finely chopped
- 2 cloves garlic, minced
- 1 lb (450g) ground turkey
- 1 teaspoon dried oregano
- 1 teaspoon dried basil
- 1/2 teaspoon smoked paprika
- Salt and pepper, to taste
- 1 cup cooked quinoa or brown rice
- 1 cup tomato sauce
- 1/2 cup shredded mozzarella cheese (optional)
- Fresh parsley or basil, chopped (for garnish)

1. Preheat Oven: Preheat your oven to 375°F (190°C).
2. Prepare Bell Peppers: Place the hollowed-out bell peppers in a baking dish, cut side up.
3. Cook Turkey Mixture:
   - In a large skillet, heat olive oil over medium heat. Add chopped onion and garlic, sautéing until softened (about 3-4 minutes).
   - Add ground turkey, breaking it up with a spoon. Cook until turkey is browned and cooked through.
   - Stir in dried oregano, dried basil, smoked paprika, salt, and pepper.
   - Add cooked quinoa or brown rice to the skillet, mixing well with the turkey mixture.
4. Stuff Bell Peppers: Spoon the turkey and quinoa mixture evenly into each bell pepper. Press down gently to pack the filling.
5. Bake: Pour tomato sauce over the stuffed peppers. Cover the baking dish with foil and bake in the preheated oven for 20 minutes.
6. Add Cheese and Finish: Remove foil and sprinkle shredded mozzarella cheese over the tops of the peppers. Return to the oven, uncovered, and bake for an additional 10 minutes, or until the cheese is melted and bubbly.
7. Serve: Remove from oven and let cool slightly. Garnish with chopped parsley or basil before serving.

Nutrition Information (per serving): Calories: 350 kcal | Protein: 30g | Carbohydrates: 30g | Fat: 12g | Fiber: 5g | Cholesterol: 75mg | Sodium: 480mg

Health Benefits: This dish provides lean protein from turkey, fiber-rich quinoa or brown rice, vitamins from bell peppers, and heart-healthy olive oil.

CHAPTER 5

BEEF, PORK, AND LAMB - MEDITERRANEAN TAKES ON MEAT DISHES

Greek Beef Souvlaki

Serves:4 | Prep Time:15 min | Cook Time:10 min

- 1 lb (450g) beef sirloin or tenderloin, cut into 1-inch cubes
- Juice of 1 lemon
- 2 tablespoons olive oil
- 2 cloves garlic, minced
- 1 teaspoon dried oregano
- 1 teaspoon dried thyme
- Salt and pepper, to taste
- 1 red onion, cut into wedges
- 1 red bell pepper, cut into chunks
- 1 yellow bell pepper, cut into chunks
- Optional: Cherry tomatoes for skewering

1. Marinate the Beef: In a bowl, combine the beef cubes with lemon juice, olive oil, minced garlic, dried oregano, dried thyme, salt, and pepper. Toss well to coat the beef evenly. Marinate for at least 15 minutes, or up to 1 hour for more flavor.
2. Prepare Skewers: If using wooden skewers, soak them in water for 10-15 minutes to prevent burning. Preheat your grill or grill pan over medium-high heat.
3. Assemble Skewers: Thread marinated beef cubes onto skewers, alternating with red onion wedges, red bell pepper chunks, yellow bell pepper chunks, and cherry tomatoes if desired.
4. Grill the Souvlaki: Place skewers on the preheated grill or grill pan. Grill for 3-4 minutes per side, or until beef is cooked to your desired doneness and vegetables are tender and slightly charred.
5. Serve: Remove skewers from the grill. Serve the souvlaki with warm pita bread or flatbread, tzatziki sauce, and a sprinkle of chopped fresh parsley or dill.

Nutrition Information (per serving): Calories: 280 kcal | Protein: 25g | Carbohydrates: 10g | Fat: 15g | Fiber: 2g | Cholesterol: 65mg | Sodium: 320mg

Health Benefits: This dish provides lean protein from beef, heart-healthy fats from olive oil, antioxidant-rich herbs, and vegetables, all of which promote satiety and support weight management within the Mediterranean Diet framework.

Spiced Lamb Koftas

Serves:4 | Prep Time:15 min | Cook Time:15 min

- 1 lb (450g) ground lamb
- 1 small onion, finely chopped
- 2 cloves garlic, minced
- 1 teaspoon ground cumin
- 1 teaspoon ground coriander
- 1/2 teaspoon smoked paprika
- 1/2 teaspoon ground cinnamon
- Salt and pepper, to taste
- 2 tablespoons chopped fresh parsley or mint
- 1 tablespoon olive oil

1. Mix the Kofta Mixture: In a large bowl, combine ground lamb, finely chopped onion, minced garlic, ground cumin, ground coriander, smoked paprika, ground cinnamon, salt, pepper, and chopped fresh parsley or mint. Mix well until all ingredients are evenly incorporated.
2. Form the Koftas: Take a portion of the mixture and shape it into elongated sausage-like shapes, about 2 inches long and 1 inch thick. Repeat with the remaining mixture, making approximately 12 koftas.
3. Cook the Koftas: Heat olive oil in a large skillet over medium heat. Add the koftas in batches, ensuring they are not overcrowded. Cook for about 3-4 minutes per side, or until browned and cooked through. You can also grill the koftas over medium-high heat for 4-5 minutes per side, if preferred.
4. Serve: Remove koftas from the skillet or grill. Serve warm with whole wheat pita bread or flatbread, tzatziki sauce, and a sprinkle of chopped fresh herbs.

Nutrition Information (per serving): Calories: 350 kcal | Protein: 25g | Carbohydrates: 3g | Fat: 27g | Fiber: 1g | Cholesterol: 85mg | Sodium: 75mg

Health Benefits: This dish provides high-quality protein from lamb, essential spices rich in antioxidants like cumin and coriander, and herbs like parsley or mint, supporting a balanced diet that aids in weight management and promotes heart health.

Pork Tenderloin with Rosemary

Serves:4 | Prep Time:10 min | Cook Time:20 min

- 1.5 lbs (680g) pork tenderloin
- Salt and pepper, to taste
- 2 tablespoons olive oil
- 4 cloves garlic, minced
- 2 tablespoons fresh rosemary, chopped (or 2 teaspoons dried rosemary)
- 1 teaspoon dried thyme
- Juice of 1 lemon
- 1/2 cup low-sodium chicken broth

1. Preheat Oven: Preheat your oven to 400°F (200°C).
2. Season Pork: Season the pork tenderloin with salt and pepper on all sides.
3. Sear Pork: In a large oven-proof skillet, heat olive oil over medium-high heat. Add the pork tenderloin and sear for 2-3 minutes on each side until browned.
4. Add Aromatics: Add minced garlic, fresh rosemary, and dried thyme to the skillet. Cook for an additional 1-2 minutes, stirring to coat the pork with the herbs and garlic.
5. Roast Pork: Pour lemon juice and chicken broth into the skillet. Transfer the skillet to the preheated oven and roast for 15-20 minutes, or until the internal temperature of the pork reaches 145°F (63°C).
6. Rest and Slice: Remove the pork from the oven and let it rest for 5 minutes before slicing.
7. Serve: Slice the pork tenderloin and drizzle with the pan juices. Serve with your favorite sides, such as roasted vegetables or a simple salad.

Nutrition Information (per serving): Calories: 280 kcal | Protein: 25g | Carbohydrates: 2g | Fat: 18g | Fiber: 0.5g | Cholesterol: 75mg | Sodium: 220mg

Health Benefits: This dish provides lean protein from pork tenderloin, heart-healthy fats from olive oil, and antioxidant-rich herbs like rosemary and thyme, supporting a balanced diet that promotes heart health and weight management within the Mediterranean Diet framework.

Beef and Eggplant Moussaka

Serves:4 | Prep Time:15 min | Cook Time:30 min

- 2 large eggplants, sliced into 1/4-inch rounds
- 1 lb lean ground beef
- 1 medium onion, finely chopped
- 2 cloves garlic, minced
- 1 can (14 oz) diced tomatoes
- 1/4 cup tomato paste
- 1/2 cup low-sodium beef broth
- 1/2 tsp ground cinnamon
- 1/2 tsp ground allspice
- 1/2 tsp ground nutmeg
- 1/2 tsp dried oregano
- 1/2 tsp dried thyme
- Salt and pepper to taste
- 1/2 cup grated Parmesan cheese
- 1/2 cup plain Greek yogurt
- 1 egg, lightly beaten
- 2 tbsp olive oil

1. Prepare the Eggplant: Preheat the oven to 400°F (200°C). Arrange the eggplant slices on a baking sheet, brush with olive oil, and season with salt and pepper. Bake for 15-20 minutes until tender and lightly browned. Remove from the oven and set aside.
2. Cook the Beef Mixture: In a large skillet over medium heat, add the remaining olive oil and sauté the onion until translucent. Add the garlic and cook for another minute. Add the ground beef and cook until browned, breaking it up with a spoon. Stir in the diced tomatoes, tomato paste, beef broth, cinnamon, allspice, nutmeg, oregano, and thyme. Season with salt and pepper to taste. Let the mixture simmer for 10 minutes, allowing the flavors to meld.
3. Assemble the Moussaka: In a medium bowl, mix the Greek yogurt, grated Parmesan cheese, and the beaten egg until well combined. In a baking dish, layer half of the eggplant slices on the bottom. Spread the beef mixture evenly over the eggplant. Layer the remaining eggplant slices on top. Pour the yogurt mixture over the top layer, spreading it evenly.
4. Bake the Moussaka: Bake in the preheated oven for 15-20 minutes, until the top is golden brown and the dish is heated through. Remove from the oven and let it rest for a few minutes before serving.

Nutritional Information (per serving): Calories: 350 | Protein: 28g | Carbohydrates: 20g | Fats: 18g | Fiber: 8g | Cholesterol: 70mg | Sodium: 420mg

Health Benefits: This Beef and Eggplant Moussaka is rich in protein and fiber. The inclusion of eggplant and tomatoes provides essential vitamins and antioxidants.

Lemon Garlic Lamb Chops

Serves:4 | Prep Time:10 min | Cook Time:20 min

- 8 lamb chops (about 1 inch thick)
- 4 cloves garlic, minced
- 1/4 cup fresh lemon juice
- 1/4 cup olive oil
- 1 tbsp fresh rosemary, chopped (or 1 tsp dried rosemary)
- 1 tsp dried oregano
- 1/2 tsp salt
- 1/4 tsp black pepper
- Lemon wedges for serving
- Fresh parsley, chopped (for garnish)

1. Prepare the Marinade: In a small bowl, mix together the minced garlic, fresh lemon juice, olive oil, rosemary, oregano, salt, and black pepper.

2. Marinate the Lamb Chops: Place the lamb chops in a large resealable plastic bag or a shallow dish. Pour the marinade over the lamb chops, ensuring they are well coated. Seal the bag or cover the dish and refrigerate for at least 30 minutes, or up to 4 hours for better flavor.

3. Cook the Lamb Chops: Preheat a grill or a large skillet over medium-high heat. Remove the lamb chops from the marinade and shake off any excess. Grill or cook the lamb chops for about 3-4 minutes per side for medium-rare, or until they reach your desired level of doneness. Let the lamb chops rest for a few minutes before serving.

4. Serve: Serve the lamb chops with lemon wedges on the side and garnish with fresh chopped parsley.

Nutritional Information (per serving): Calories: 350 | Protein: 25g | Carbohydrates: 2g | Fats: 28g | Fiber: 0g | Cholesterol: 85mg | Sodium: 350mg

Health Benefits: These Lemon Garlic Lamb Chops are rich in protein and healthy fats, which can help support muscle growth and overall health. The use of olive oil and fresh herbs adds a Mediterranean flair, providing antioxidants and anti-inflammatory benefits.

Mediterranean Beef Stew

Serves:4 | Prep Time:10 min | Cook Time:30 min

- 1 lb lean beef stew meat, cut into 1-inch cubes
- 2 tbsp olive oil
- 1 large onion, chopped
- 3 cloves garlic, minced
- 2 large carrots, sliced
- 1 large bell pepper, chopped
- 1 can (14 oz) diced tomatoes
- 1 cup low-sodium beef broth
- 1/2 cup dry red wine (optional)
- 1 tsp dried oregano
- 1 tsp dried thyme
- 1/2 tsp ground cumin
- 1/2 tsp paprika
- 1/2 tsp salt
- 1/4 tsp black pepper
- 1 bay leaf
- 1/2 cup chopped fresh parsley (for garnish)

1. Sear the Beef: Heat the olive oil in a large skillet or Dutch oven over medium-high heat. Add the beef cubes and sear on all sides until browned. Remove the beef and set aside.

2. Sauté the Vegetables: In the same skillet, add the chopped onion, garlic, carrots, and bell pepper.

Sauté for about 5 minutes until the vegetables are softened.

3. Combine Ingredients: Return the seared beef to the skillet. Add the diced tomatoes, beef broth, red wine (if using), oregano, thyme, cumin, paprika, salt, black pepper, and bay leaf. Stir well to combine.

4. Simmer the Stew: Bring the mixture to a boil, then reduce the heat to low. Cover and simmer for about 20 minutes, or until the beef is tender and the flavors have melded together. Remove the bay leaf before serving.

5. Serve: Ladle the stew into bowls and garnish with fresh chopped parsley.

Nutritional Information (per serving): Calories: 320 | Protein: 28g | Carbohydrates: 15g | Fats: 18g | Fiber: 4g | Cholesterol: 70mg | Sodium: 350mg

Health Benefits: This Mediterranean Beef Stew is rich in protein and fiber, promoting muscle health and digestive well-being. The use of olive oil and vegetables provides essential nutrients and antioxidants, supporting heart health and overall wellness.

Pork and Fennel Sausage Patties

Serves:4 | Prep Time:10 min | Cook Time:20 min

- 1 lb ground pork (preferably lean)
- 1 small fennel bulb, finely chopped
- 1 small onion, finely chopped
- 2 cloves garlic, minced
- 1 tsp fennel seeds, crushed
- 1 tsp dried oregano
- 1/2 tsp dried thyme
- 1/2 tsp ground black pepper
- 1/2 tsp salt
- 1/4 cup fresh parsley, chopped
- 1 tbsp olive oil (for cooking)

1. Prepare the Mixture: In a large bowl, combine the ground pork, chopped fennel bulb, onion, garlic, crushed fennel seeds, oregano, thyme, black pepper, salt, and fresh parsley. Mix well until all the ingredients are evenly distributed.

2. Form the Patties: Divide the mixture into 8 equal portions and shape each portion into a patty.

3. Cook the Patties: Heat the olive oil in a large skillet over medium heat. Add the patties to the skillet and cook for about 4-5 minutes on each side, or until they are browned and cooked through. Ensure the internal temperature of the patties reaches 160°F (71°C).

4. Serve: Serve the sausage patties with a side of fresh salad, roasted vegetables, or whole-grain bread.

Nutritional Information (per serving): Calories: 250 | Protein: 20g | Carbohydrates: 5g |

Fats: 18g | Fiber: 1g | Cholesterol: 60mg | Sodium: 450mg

Health Benefits: These Pork and Fennel Sausage Patties are high in protein and flavor, while the fennel provides dietary fiber and antioxidants, supporting digestive health and overall well-being.

Herb-Crusted Lamb Roast

Serves:6 | Prep Time:15 min | Cook Time:25 min

- 3 lb boneless leg of lamb
- 3 cloves garlic, minced
- 2 tbsp fresh rosemary, chopped
- 2 tbsp fresh thyme, chopped
- 2 tbsp fresh parsley, chopped
- 1 tbsp Dijon mustard
- 1 tbsp olive oil
- 1 tsp salt
- 1/2 tsp black pepper

1. Preheat your oven to 425°F (220°C).
2. Prepare the Herb Mixture: In a small bowl, combine the minced garlic, rosemary, thyme, parsley, Dijon mustard, olive oil, salt, and black pepper.
3. Prepare the Lamb: Pat the lamb dry with paper towels. Rub the herb mixture all over the lamb, ensuring it is evenly coated.
4. Roast the Lamb: Place the lamb on a roasting rack in a roasting pan. Roast in the preheated oven for about 25 minutes, or until the internal temperature reaches 135°F (57°C) for medium-rare. Adjust cooking time based on desired doneness (use a meat thermometer for accuracy).
5. Rest and Serve: Remove the lamb from the oven and let it rest for 10 minutes before slicing. Serve with roasted vegetables or a fresh salad.

Nutritional Information (per serving): Calories: 350 | Protein: 32g | Carbohydrates: 2g | Fats: 22g | Fiber: 0g | Cholesterol: 110mg | Sodium: 480mg

Health Benefits: This Herb-Crusted Lamb Roast is rich in protein and healthy fats, which are essential for muscle repair and overall health. The fresh herbs provide antioxidants and anti-inflammatory properties, enhancing the dish's flavor and health benefits.

Greek-Style Stuffed Peppers

Serves:4 | Prep Time:15 min | Cook Time:30 min

- 4 large bell peppers, tops cut off and seeds removed
- 1 lb lean ground beef or turkey
- 1/2 cup cooked quinoa
- 1 small onion, finely chopped
- 2 cloves garlic, minced
- 1 can (14 oz) diced tomatoes, drained
- 1/2 cup crumbled feta cheese
- 1/4 cup chopped fresh parsley
- 1 tsp dried oregano
- 1/2 tsp ground cumin
- 1/2 tsp salt
- 1/4 tsp black pepper
- 2 tbsp olive oil

1. Preheat oven to 375°F (190°C).
2. Heat 1 tbsp olive oil in a skillet over medium heat. Sauté onion and garlic until soft. Add ground beef or turkey and cook until browned. Stir in quinoa, tomatoes, feta, parsley, oregano, cumin, salt, and pepper.
3. Drizzle the inside of each pepper with remaining olive oil. Fill each pepper with the meat mixture.
4. Place stuffed peppers in a baking dish. Cover with foil and bake for 20 minutes. Remove foil and bake for another 10 minutes.
5. Serve hot, garnished with extra parsley if desired.

Nutritional Information (per serving): Calories: 320 | Protein: 25g | Carbohydrates: 18g | Fats: 18g | Fiber: 5g | Cholesterol: 60mg | Sodium: 450mg

Health Benefits: These Greek-Style Stuffed Peppers are packed with protein and fiber, promoting satiety and supporting muscle health. The combination of lean meat, quinoa, and fresh vegetables provides a balanced meal rich in essential nutrients and antioxidants, aligning with the health benefits of the Mediterranean Diet.

Beef and Olive Tagine

Serves:4 | Prep Time:15 min | Cook Time:30 min

- 1 lb lean beef stew meat, cut into 1-inch cubes
- 2 tbsp olive oil
- 1 large onion, chopped
- 3 cloves garlic, minced
- 1 cup green olives, pitted
- 1 can (14 oz) diced tomatoes
- 1/2 cup low-sodium beef broth
- 1/4 cup dried apricots, chopped
- 1 tsp ground cumin
- 1 tsp ground cinnamon
- 1 tsp ground coriander
- 1/2 tsp ground turmeric
- 1/2 tsp ground ginger
- 1/2 tsp salt
- 1/4 tsp black pepper
- 1/4 cup fresh cilantro, chopped (for garnish)
- 1/4 cup fresh parsley, chopped (for garnish)

1. Heat 1 tablespoon of olive oil in a large skillet or Dutch oven over medium-high heat. Add the beef cubes and sear on all sides until browned. Remove the beef and set aside.

2. In the same skillet, add the remaining olive oil and sauté the chopped onion until softened. Add the minced garlic and cook for another minute.
3. Return the beef to the skillet. Add the diced tomatoes, beef broth, olives, dried apricots, cumin, cinnamon, coriander, turmeric, ginger, salt, and black pepper. Stir well to combine.
4. Bring the mixture to a boil, then reduce the heat to low. Cover and simmer for about 20 minutes, or until the beef is tender and the flavors have melded together.
5. Serve hot, garnished with fresh cilantro and parsley.

Nutritional Information (per serving): Calories: 340 | Protein: 28g | Carbohydrates: 18g | Fats: 18g | Fiber: 4g | Cholesterol: 70mg | Sodium: 450mg

Health Benefits: This Beef and Olive Tagine is rich in protein and fiber, promoting muscle health and digestive well-being. The combination of lean beef, olives, and fresh herbs provides a balanced meal with essential nutrients and antioxidants, supporting heart health and overall wellness.

Balsamic Glazed Pork Chops

Serves:4 | Prep Time:10 min | Cook Time:20 min

- 4 boneless pork chops (about 1 inch thick)
- 1/4 cup balsamic vinegar
- 2 tbsp honey
- 2 cloves garlic, minced
- 1 tbsp olive oil
- 1 tsp dried thyme
- 1/2 tsp salt
- 1/4 tsp black pepper
- Fresh parsley, chopped (for garnish)

1. In a small bowl, mix the balsamic vinegar, honey, minced garlic, dried thyme, salt, and black pepper.
2. Heat the olive oil in a large skillet over medium-high heat. Add the pork chops and cook for about 4-5 minutes on each side, or until they are browned and cooked through. Remove the pork chops and set aside.
3. In the same skillet, pour the balsamic mixture and bring it to a boil. Reduce the heat and simmer for about 2-3 minutes, or until the glaze has thickened.
4. Return the pork chops to the skillet, turning them to coat with the glaze.
5. Serve the pork chops hot, garnished with fresh parsley.

Nutritional Information (per serving): Calories: 300 | Protein: 25g | Carbohydrates: 15g | Fats: 16g | Fiber: 0g | Cholesterol: 70mg | Sodium: 400mg

Health Benefits: These Balsamic Glazed Pork Chops are rich in protein, supporting muscle health. The balsamic vinegar and garlic add antioxidants, promoting heart health and overall wellness. This dish is a great example of the Mediterranean Diet's balance of lean proteins and flavorful ingredients.

Slow-Cooked Lamb Shanks

Serves:4 | Prep Time:15 min | Cook Time:30 min

- 4 lamb shanks
- 2 tbsp olive oil
- 1 large onion, chopped
- 4 cloves garlic, minced
- 2 large carrots, chopped
- 2 celery stalks, chopped
- 1 can (14 oz) diced tomatoes
- 1 cup low-sodium beef broth
- 1/2 cup dry red wine (optional)
- 1 tbsp tomato paste
- 1 tsp dried rosemary
- 1 tsp dried thyme
- 1 tsp ground cumin
- 1/2 tsp ground cinnamon
- 1/2 tsp salt
- 1/4 tsp black pepper
- Fresh parsley, chopped (for garnish)

1. Heat 1 tablespoon of olive oil in a large skillet over medium-high heat. Add the lamb shanks and sear on all sides until browned. Remove the lamb and set aside.
2. In the same skillet, add the remaining olive oil and sauté the chopped onion, garlic, carrots, and celery until softened.
3. Transfer the sautéed vegetables to a slow cooker. Add the seared lamb shanks, diced tomatoes, beef broth, red wine (if using), tomato paste, rosemary, thyme, cumin, cinnamon, salt, and black pepper. Stir well to combine.
4. Cover and cook on low for 6-8 hours, or until the lamb shanks are tender and the meat is falling off the bone.
5. Serve hot, garnished with fresh parsley.

Nutritional Information (per serving): Calories: 450 | Protein: 35g | Carbohydrates: 18g | Fats: 28g | Fiber: 4g | Cholesterol: 110mg | Sodium: 500mg

Health Benefits: These Slow-Cooked Lamb Shanks are rich in protein and healthy fats, supporting muscle health and overall wellness. The use of fresh vegetables and herbs provides essential nutrients and antioxidants, promoting heart health and aligning with the Mediterranean Diet.

Mediterranean Meatloaf

Serves:6 | Prep Time:15 min | Cook Time:30 min

- 1 lb lean ground beef
- 1/2 lb ground turkey
- 1 small onion, finely chopped
- 2 cloves garlic, minced
- 1/2 cup breadcrumbs (whole wheat preferred)
- 1/4 cup milk (or almond milk for dairy-free)
- 1 egg, lightly beaten
- 1/4 cup crumbled feta cheese
- 1/4 cup chopped sun-dried tomatoes
- 1/4 cup chopped fresh parsley
- 1 tbsp dried oregano
- 1 tsp dried basil
- 1/2 tsp salt
- 1/4 tsp black pepper
- 1/4 cup tomato paste

1. Preheat oven to 375°F (190°C).
2. In a large bowl, combine the ground beef, ground turkey, onion, garlic, breadcrumbs, milk, egg, feta cheese, sun-dried tomatoes, parsley, oregano, basil, salt, and black pepper. Mix well until all ingredients are evenly incorporated.
3. Transfer the mixture to a loaf pan, pressing down gently to shape it into a loaf. Spread the tomato paste evenly over the top.
4. Bake in the preheated oven for 30-35 minutes, or until the meatloaf is cooked through and the internal temperature reaches 160°F (71°C).
5. Let the meatloaf rest for a few minutes before slicing. Serve hot.

Nutritional Information (per serving): Calories: 280 | Protein: 24g | Carbohydrates: 12g | Fats: 14g | Fiber: 2g | Cholesterol: 80mg | Sodium: 450mg

Health Benefits: This Mediterranean Meatloaf is high in protein and low in fat, supporting muscle health and weight management. The inclusion of feta cheese, sun-dried tomatoes, and fresh herbs adds flavor and essential nutrients, promoting overall wellness and heart health.

Spiced Beef Kebabs

Serves:4 | Prep Time:15 min | Cook Time:15 min

- 1 lb lean beef, cut into 1-inch cubes
- 2 tbsp olive oil
- 2 cloves garlic, minced
- 1 tsp ground cumin
- 1 tsp ground coriander
- 1 tsp paprika
- 1/2 tsp ground cinnamon
- 1/2 tsp ground allspice
- 1/2 tsp salt
- 1/4 tsp black pepper
- 1 red bell pepper, cut into 1-inch pieces
- 1 yellow bell pepper, cut into 1-inch pieces
- 1 red onion, cut into wedges
- Fresh parsley, chopped (for garnish)
- Lemon wedges (for serving)

1. In a large bowl, combine the olive oil, garlic, cumin, coriander, paprika, cinnamon, allspice, salt, and black pepper. Add the beef cubes and toss to coat evenly. Cover and marinate in the refrigerator for at least 30 minutes, or up to 2 hours for better flavor.
2. Preheat the grill or a grill pan over medium-high heat.
3. Thread the marinated beef, bell peppers, and onion onto skewers, alternating between the meat and vegetables.
4. Grill the kebabs for about 10-12 minutes, turning occasionally, until the beef is cooked to your desired doneness and the vegetables are tender and slightly charred.
5. Serve hot, garnished with fresh parsley and lemon wedges on the side.

Nutritional Information (per serving): Calories: 300 | Protein: 25g | Carbohydrates: 10g | Fats: 18g | Fiber: 3g | Cholesterol: 70mg | Sodium: 450mg

Health Benefits: These Spiced Beef Kebabs are high in protein and packed with flavorful spices that provide antioxidants and anti-inflammatory properties. The inclusion of fresh vegetables adds essential vitamins and minerals, making this dish a balanced and nutritious option that supports overall health and wellness.

Pork and Chickpea Stew

Serves:4 | Prep Time:15 min | Cook Time:30 min

- 1 lb lean pork, cut into 1-inch cubes
- 2 tbsp olive oil
- 1 large onion, chopped
- 3 cloves garlic, minced
- 2 large carrots, chopped
- 1 red bell pepper, chopped
- 1 can (14 oz) diced tomatoes
- 1 can (14 oz) chickpeas, drained and rinsed
- 1 cup low-sodium chicken broth
- 1 tsp ground cumin
- 1 tsp smoked paprika
- 1/2 tsp ground coriander
- 1/2 tsp dried thyme
- 1/2 tsp salt
- 1/4 tsp black pepper
- 1/4 cup fresh parsley, chopped (for garnish)

1. Heat 1 tablespoon of olive oil in a large skillet or Dutch oven over medium-high heat. Add the pork cubes and sear on all sides until browned. Remove the pork and set aside.
2. In the same skillet, add the remaining olive oil and sauté the chopped onion, garlic, carrots, and red bell pepper until softened.
3. Return the pork to the skillet. Add the diced tomatoes, chickpeas, chicken broth, cumin, smoked paprika, coriander, thyme, salt, and black pepper. Stir well to combine.
4. Bring the mixture to a boil, then reduce the heat to low. Cover and simmer for about 20 minutes, or until the pork is tender and the flavors have melded together.
5. Serve hot, garnished with fresh parsley.

Nutritional Information (per serving): Calories: 350 | Protein: 28g | Carbohydrates: 25g | Fats: 16g | Fiber: 8g | Cholesterol: 70mg | Sodium: 400mg

Health Benefits: This Pork and Chickpea Stew is high in protein and fiber, promoting muscle health and digestive well-being. The combination of lean pork, chickpeas, and fresh vegetables provides a balanced meal rich in essential nutrients and antioxidants, supporting overall health and wellness.

CHAPTER 6

FISH AND SEAFOOD - FRESH AND HEART-HEALTHY SEAFOOD RECIPES

Lemon Garlic Grilled Shrimp

Serves:4 | Prep Time:10 min | Cook Time:10 min

- 1 lb large shrimp, peeled and deveined
- 3 cloves garlic, minced
- 1/4 cup fresh lemon juice
- 2 tbsp olive oil
- 1 tbsp fresh parsley, chopped
- 1 tsp dried oregano
- 1/2 tsp salt
- 1/4 tsp black pepper
- Lemon wedges (for serving)

1. In a large bowl, combine the minced garlic, lemon juice, olive oil, parsley, oregano, salt, and black pepper. Add the shrimp and toss to coat. Marinate for 15-20 minutes.
2. Preheat the grill or grill pan over medium-high heat.
3. Thread the shrimp onto skewers (if using wooden skewers, soak them in water for 30 minutes beforehand).
4. Grill the shrimp for about 2-3 minutes per side, or until they are pink and opaque.
5. Serve hot with lemon wedges on the side.

Nutritional Information (per serving): Calories: 200 | Protein: 25g | Carbohydrates: 2g | Fats: 10g | Fiber: 0g | Cholesterol: 170mg | Sodium: 600mg

Health Benefits: This Lemon Garlic Grilled Shrimp is high in protein and low in calories, making it a great option for muscle health and weight management. The lemon juice and garlic provide antioxidants and support immune function, while the olive oil offers heart-healthy fats. This dish aligns perfectly with the Mediterranean Diet's emphasis on fresh, flavorful ingredients.

Mediterranean Baked Salmon

Serves:4 | Prep Time:10 min | Cook Time:20 min

- 4 salmon fillets (about 6 oz each)
- 3 cloves garlic, minced
- 1/4 cup olive oil
- 2 tbsp fresh lemon juice
- 1 tsp dried oregano
- 1 tsp dried thyme
- 1/2 tsp salt
- 1/4 tsp black pepper
- 1 cup cherry tomatoes, halved
- 1/4 cup kalamata olives, pitted and sliced
- 1/4 cup crumbled feta cheese
- Fresh parsley, chopped (for garnish)
- Lemon wedges (for serving)
- Instructions:
- Preheat your oven to 400°F (200°C).

1. In a small bowl, mix the minced garlic, olive oil, lemon juice, oregano, thyme, salt, and black pepper.
2. Place the salmon fillets on a baking sheet lined with parchment paper. Brush the garlic and olive oil mixture over the salmon fillets.
3. Scatter the cherry tomatoes, kalamata olives, and crumbled feta cheese around the salmon on the baking sheet.
4. Bake in the preheated oven for 15-20 minutes, or until the salmon is cooked through and flakes easily with a fork.
5. Serve hot, garnished with fresh parsley and lemon wedges on the side.

Nutritional Information (per serving): Calories: 350 | Protein: 30g | Carbohydrates: 5g | Fats: 22g | Fiber: 1g | Cholesterol: 80mg | Sodium: 450mg

Health Benefits: This Mediterranean Baked Salmon is rich in omega-3 fatty acids, supporting heart health and reducing inflammation. The combination of fresh vegetables, olives, and olive oil provides essential vitamins, minerals, and antioxidants, promoting overall wellness and aligning with the principles of the Mediterranean Diet.

Spicy Fish Tacos

Serves:4 | Prep Time:15 min | Cook Time:15 min

- 1 lb white fish fillets (such as cod or tilapia)
- 2 tbsp olive oil
- 1 tsp chili powder
- 1 tsp cumin
- 1/2 tsp paprika
- 1/2 tsp garlic powder
- 1/4 tsp cayenne pepper (optional for extra spice)
- 1/2 tsp salt
- 1/4 tsp black pepper
- 8 small corn tortillas

- 1 cup shredded lettuce
- 1/2 cup diced tomatoes
- 1/4 cup diced red onion
- 1/4 cup chopped fresh cilantro
- 1 avocado, sliced
- Lime wedges (for serving)

1. In a small bowl, mix the chili powder, cumin, paprika, garlic powder, cayenne pepper (if using), salt, and black pepper.
2. Rub the spice mixture evenly over the fish fillets.
3. Heat the olive oil in a large skillet over medium-high heat. Add the fish fillets and cook for about 3-4 minutes per side, or until the fish is cooked through and flakes easily with a fork. Remove from heat and break into bite-sized pieces.
4. Warm the corn tortillas in a dry skillet or in the oven.
5. Assemble the tacos by placing some shredded lettuce, diced tomatoes, red onion, and cilantro on each tortilla. Top with the cooked fish and avocado slices.
6. Serve immediately with lime wedges on the side.

Nutritional Information (per serving): Calories: 300 | Protein: 25g | Carbohydrates: 20g | Fats: 12g | Fiber: 5g | Cholesterol: 55mg | Sodium: 400mg

Health Benefits: These Spicy Fish Tacos are high in protein and healthy fats, supporting muscle health and overall wellness. The fresh vegetables and spices provide essential vitamins, minerals, and antioxidants, promoting digestive health and aligning with the Mediterranean Diet's emphasis on fresh, flavorful ingredients.

Greek-Style Grilled Octopus

Serves:4 | Prep Time:15 min | Cook Time:30 min

- 2 lbs octopus, cleaned
- 1/4 cup olive oil
- 3 cloves garlic, minced
- 2 tbsp fresh lemon juice
- 1 tsp dried oregano
- 1/2 tsp dried thyme
- 1/2 tsp salt
- 1/4 tsp black pepper
- Fresh parsley, chopped (for garnish)
- Lemon wedges (for serving)

1. Bring a large pot of water to a boil. Add the octopus and simmer for 30 minutes until tender. Drain and let it cool slightly.
2. In a large bowl, combine the olive oil, minced garlic, lemon juice, oregano, thyme, salt, and black pepper.
3. Cut the octopus into serving-size pieces and add them to the marinade.

Toss to coat and let marinate for at least 1 hour, or up to overnight in the refrigerator.
4. Preheat the grill or grill pan over medium-high heat.
5. Grill the marinated octopus for about 3-4 minutes per side, until it is nicely charred and heated through.
6. Serve hot, garnished with fresh parsley and lemon wedges on the side.

Nutritional Information (per serving): Calories: 250 | Protein: 25g | Carbohydrates: 2g | Fats: 15g | Fiber: 0g | Cholesterol: 95mg | Sodium: 400mg

Health Benefits: This Greek-Style Grilled Octopus is rich in protein and low in carbohydrates, making it an excellent choice for muscle health and weight management.

Tuna and White Bean Salad

Serves:4 | Prep Time:10 min | Cook Time:0 min

- 2 cans (5 oz each) tuna packed in water, drained
- 1 can (15 oz) white beans (cannellini or great northern), drained and rinsed
- 1 small red onion, finely chopped
- 1 cup cherry tomatoes, halved
- 1/4 cup fresh parsley, chopped
- 2 tbsp capers, drained
- 1/4 cup olive oil
- 2 tbsp fresh lemon juice
- 1 tsp dried oregano
- Salt and pepper to taste
- Mixed greens (optional, for serving)

1. In a large bowl, combine the drained tuna, white beans, red onion, cherry tomatoes, parsley, and capers.
2. In a small bowl, whisk together the olive oil, lemon juice, dried oregano, salt, and pepper.
3. Pour the dressing over the tuna and bean mixture and toss gently to combine.
4. Serve the salad on its own or over a bed of mixed greens.

Nutritional Information (per serving): Calories: 250 | Protein: 20g | Carbohydrates: 18g | Fats: 12g | Fiber: 5g | Cholesterol: 20mg | Sodium: 400mg

Health Benefits: This Tuna and White Bean Salad is high in protein and fiber, promoting muscle health and digestive wellness. The use of olive oil and fresh vegetables provides essential nutrients and antioxidants, supporting heart health and overall well-being. This dish aligns perfectly with the Mediterranean Diet's emphasis on fresh, wholesome ingredients.

Lemon Herb Cod Fillets

Serves:4 | Prep Time:10 min | Cook Time:20 min

- 4 cod fillets (about 6 oz each)
- 3 tbsp olive oil
- 3 cloves garlic, minced
- 2 tbsp fresh lemon juice
- 1 tsp lemon zest
- 1 tsp dried oregano
- 1 tsp dried thyme
- 1/2 tsp salt
- 1/4 tsp black pepper
- Fresh parsley, chopped (for garnish)
- Lemon wedges (for serving)

1. Preheat your oven to 400°F (200°C).
2. In a small bowl, combine the olive oil, minced garlic, lemon juice, lemon zest, oregano, thyme, salt, and black pepper.
3. Place the cod fillets on a baking sheet lined with parchment paper. Brush the lemon herb mixture over the fillets, coating them evenly.
4. Bake in the preheated oven for 15-20 minutes, or until the cod is cooked through and flakes easily with a fork.
5. Serve hot, garnished with fresh parsley and lemon wedges on the side.

Nutritional Information (per serving): Calories: 250 | Protein: 30g | Carbohydrates: 2g | Fats: 12g | Fiber: 0g | Cholesterol: 70mg | Sodium: 400mg

Health Benefits: These Lemon Herb Cod Fillets are rich in lean protein and low in calories, making them an excellent choice for muscle health and weight management. The olive oil and fresh herbs provide heart-healthy fats and antioxidants, supporting overall wellness and aligning with the Mediterranean Diet's principles of using fresh, nutritious ingredients.

Mediterranean Seafood Paella

Serves:4 | Prep Time:15 min | Cook Time:30 min

- 2 tbsp olive oil
- 1 onion, finely chopped
- 3 cloves garlic, minced
- 1 red bell pepper, chopped
- 1 cup Arborio rice
- 1 can (14 oz) diced tomatoes, drained
- 3 cups low-sodium chicken or seafood broth
- 1/2 cup dry white wine (optional)
- 1 tsp smoked paprika
- 1/2 tsp saffron threads (optional)
- 1/2 tsp salt
- 1/4 tsp black pepper
- 1/2 lb shrimp, peeled and deveined
- 1/2 lb mussels, cleaned
- 1/2 lb squid, cleaned and cut into rings
- 1/4 cup frozen peas
- 1/4 cup chopped fresh parsley
- Lemon wedges (for serving)

1. Heat the olive oil in a large, deep skillet or paella pan over medium heat. Add the chopped onion and garlic, and sauté until softened.
2. Add the red bell pepper and Arborio rice, stirring to coat the rice with oil. Cook for 2-3 minutes.
3. Stir in the diced tomatoes, broth, white wine (if using), smoked paprika, saffron (if using), salt, and black pepper. Bring to a boil.
4. Reduce the heat to low and simmer, uncovered, for about 15 minutes, stirring occasionally, until the rice is partially cooked.
5. Arrange the shrimp, mussels, and squid over the rice. Sprinkle the peas on top. Cover and cook for an additional 10-15 minutes, or until the seafood is cooked and the rice is tender.
6. Remove from heat and let the paella rest for a few minutes. Garnish with fresh parsley and serve with lemon wedges on the side.

Nutritional Information (per serving): Calories: 400 | Protein: 30g | Carbohydrates: 45g | Fats: 12g | Fiber: 4g | Cholesterol: 150mg | Sodium: 600mg

Health Benefits: This Mediterranean Seafood Paella is rich in lean protein and healthy fats, promoting muscle health and heart wellness. The variety of seafood provides essential omega-3 fatty acids and antioxidants, while the vegetables add important vitamins and minerals, supporting overall health and aligning with the principles of the Mediterranean Diet.

Garlic Butter Shrimp Skewers

Serves:4 | Prep Time:15 min | Cook Time:10 min

- 1 lb large shrimp, peeled and deveined
- 3 tbsp unsalted butter, melted
- 3 cloves garlic, minced
- 2 tbsp fresh lemon juice
- 1 tbsp olive oil
- 1 tsp dried oregano
- 1/2 tsp paprika
- 1/2 tsp salt
- 1/4 tsp black pepper
- Fresh parsley, chopped (for garnish)
- Lemon wedges (for serving)

1. Preheat the grill or grill pan over medium-high heat.
2. In a large bowl, combine the melted butter, minced garlic, lemon juice, olive oil, oregano, paprika, salt, and black pepper. Add the shrimp and toss to coat evenly.
3. Thread the shrimp onto skewers (if using wooden skewers, soak them in water for 30 minutes beforehand).
4. Grill the shrimp skewers for about 2-3 minutes per side, or until the shrimp are pink and opaque.

5. Serve hot, garnished with fresh parsley and lemon wedges on the side.

Nutritional Information (per serving): Calories: 250 | Protein: 25g | Carbohydrates: 2g | Fats: 15g | Fiber: 0g | Cholesterol: 170mg | Sodium: 600mg

Health Benefits:
These Garlic Butter Shrimp Skewers are high in protein and healthy fats, supporting muscle health and overall wellness. The garlic and lemon provide antioxidants and support immune function, while the olive oil offers heart-healthy fats. This dish aligns perfectly with the Mediterranean Diet's emphasis on fresh, flavorful ingredients.

Grilled Sardines with Lemon

Serves:4 | Prep Time:10 min | Cook Time:10 min

- 8 fresh sardines, cleaned and gutted
- 3 tbsp olive oil
- 3 cloves garlic, minced
- 2 tbsp fresh lemon juice
- 1 tsp lemon zest
- 1 tsp dried oregano
- 1/2 tsp salt
- 1/4 tsp black pepper
- Fresh parsley, chopped (for garnish)
- Lemon wedges (for serving)

1. Preheat the grill or grill pan over medium-high heat.
2. In a small bowl, combine the olive oil, minced garlic, lemon juice, lemon zest, oregano, salt, and black pepper.
3. Brush the sardines with the olive oil mixture, coating them evenly.
4. Grill the sardines for about 3-4 minutes per side, or until they are cooked through and have a nice char.
5. Serve hot, garnished with fresh parsley and lemon wedges on the side.

Nutritional Information (per serving): Calories: 200 | Protein: 25g | Carbohydrates: 2g | Fats: 10g | Fiber: 0g | Cholesterol: 70mg | Sodium: 300mg

Health Benefits: These Grilled Sardines with Lemon are rich in omega-3 fatty acids, supporting heart health and reducing inflammation. The combination of fresh herbs, lemon, and olive oil provides essential nutrients and antioxidants, promoting overall wellness and aligning with the Mediterranean Diet's principles of using fresh, nutritious ingredients.

Baked Stuffed Clams

Serves:4 | Prep Time:20 min | Cook Time:15 min

- 12 large clams, cleaned and shucked (save the shells)
- 2 tbsp olive oil
- 1/2 cup bread crumbs (whole wheat preferred)
- 3 cloves garlic, minced
- 1/4 cup fresh parsley, chopped
- 1/4 cup grated Parmesan cheese
- 2 tbsp lemon juice
- 1 tsp lemon zest
- 1 tsp dried oregano
- 1/2 tsp salt
- 1/4 tsp black pepper
- Lemon wedges (for serving)

1. Preheat your oven to 400°F (200°C).
2. In a medium skillet, heat the olive oil over medium heat. Add the minced garlic and sauté until fragrant, about 1 minute.
3. Add the bread crumbs to the skillet and cook, stirring frequently, until they are golden brown and crispy.
4. Remove the skillet from the heat and stir in the chopped parsley, grated Parmesan cheese, lemon juice, lemon zest, oregano, salt, and black pepper.
5. Place the clam shells on a baking sheet. Spoon the bread crumb mixture into each shell, pressing it down gently to pack it in.
6. Bake in the preheated oven for 10-15 minutes, or until the topping is golden brown and the clams are cooked through.
7. Serve hot with lemon wedges on the side.

Nutritional Information (per serving): Calories: 200 | Protein: 12g | Carbohydrates: 15g | Fats: 10g | Fiber: 1g | Cholesterol: 30mg | Sodium: 400mg

Health Benefits: These Baked Stuffed Clams are rich in protein and essential minerals like iron and zinc, supporting overall health and immune function. The combination of whole wheat bread crumbs, fresh herbs, and olive oil provides heart-healthy fats and antioxidants, aligning with the Mediterranean Diet's emphasis on fresh, nutritious ingredients.

Mediterranean Fish Stew

Serves:4 | Prep Time:15 min | Cook Time:30 min

- 2 tbsp olive oil
- 1 large onion, chopped
- 3 cloves garlic, minced
- 1 red bell pepper, chopped
- 1 yellow bell pepper, chopped
- 1 can (14 oz) diced tomatoes
- 2 cups low-sodium vegetable or fish broth
- 1/2 cup dry white wine (optional)

- 1 tsp smoked paprika
- 1 tsp dried thyme
- 1/2 tsp dried oregano
- 1/2 tsp salt
- 1/4 tsp black pepper
- 1 lb white fish fillets (such as cod or haddock), cut into 1-inch pieces
- 1/2 lb shrimp, peeled and deveined
- 1/2 cup chopped fresh parsley
- Lemon wedges (for serving)

1. Heat the olive oil in a large pot over medium heat. Add the chopped onion and garlic, and sauté until softened.
2. Add the red and yellow bell peppers and cook for another 5 minutes.
3. Stir in the diced tomatoes, vegetable or fish broth, white wine (if using), smoked paprika, thyme, oregano, salt, and black pepper. Bring to a boil.
4. Reduce the heat to low and simmer for about 15 minutes, allowing the flavors to meld.
5. Add the fish pieces and shrimp to the pot. Cook for an additional 5-7 minutes, or until the seafood is cooked through.
6. Stir in the chopped fresh parsley just before serving.
7. Serve hot with lemon wedges on the side.

Nutritional Information (per serving): Calories: 300 | Protein: 30g | Carbohydrates: 15g | Fats: 12g | Fiber: 3g | Cholesterol: 150mg | Sodium: 500mg

Health Benefits: This Mediterranean Fish Stew is rich in lean protein and healthy fats, promoting muscle health and heart wellness. The variety of seafood provides essential omega-3 fatty acids and antioxidants, while the vegetables add important vitamins and minerals, supporting overall health and aligning with the principles of the Mediterranean Diet.

Spicy Calamari Salad

Serves:4 | Prep Time:15 min | Cook Time:10 min

- 1 lb calamari (squid), cleaned and cut into rings
- 2 tbsp olive oil
- 2 cloves garlic, minced
- 1 red chili, finely chopped (adjust to taste)
- 1 tsp smoked paprika
- 1/2 tsp ground cumin
- 1/2 tsp salt
- 1/4 tsp black pepper
- 1 cup cherry tomatoes, halved
- 1/2 red onion, thinly sliced
- 1 cucumber, thinly sliced
- 1/4 cup fresh parsley, chopped
- 1/4 cup fresh cilantro, chopped
- 2 tbsp fresh lemon juice
- 1 tbsp red wine vinegar

1. Heat 1 tablespoon of olive oil in a large skillet over medium-high heat. Add the minced garlic and chopped red chili, and sauté for 1-2 minutes until fragrant.
2. Add the calamari rings to the skillet and cook for 3-4 minutes, or until the calamari is opaque and tender. Remove from heat and set aside.
3. In a large bowl, combine the cherry tomatoes, red onion, cucumber, parsley, and cilantro.
4. In a small bowl, whisk together the remaining olive oil, lemon juice, red wine vinegar, smoked paprika, cumin, salt, and black pepper.
5. Add the cooked calamari to the bowl with the vegetables. Pour the dressing over the salad and toss gently to combine.
6. Serve immediately, garnished with additional fresh herbs if desired.

Nutritional Information (per serving):
Calories: 220 | Protein: 20g | Carbohydrates: 10g | Fats: 12g | Fiber: 2g | Cholesterol: 250mg | Sodium: 500mg

Health Benefits: This Spicy Calamari Salad is rich in lean protein and low in calories, making it an excellent choice for muscle health and weight management. The fresh vegetables and herbs provide essential vitamins, minerals, and antioxidants, supporting overall wellness and aligning with the Mediterranean Diet's principles of using fresh, nutritious ingredients.

Herb-Crusted Sea Bass

Serves:4 | Prep Time:10 min | Cook Time:20 min

- 4 sea bass fillets (about 6 oz each)
- 1/4 cup olive oil
- 3 cloves garlic, minced
- 2 tbsp fresh lemon juice
- 1 tbsp lemon zest
- 2 tbsp fresh parsley, chopped
- 2 tbsp fresh thyme, chopped
- 1 tbsp fresh rosemary, chopped
- 1/2 tsp salt
- 1/4 tsp black pepper
- Lemon wedges (for serving)

1. Preheat your oven to 400°F (200°C).
2. In a small bowl, combine the olive oil, minced garlic, lemon juice, lemon zest, parsley, thyme, rosemary, salt, and black pepper.
3. Place the sea bass fillets on a baking sheet lined with parchment paper. Brush the herb mixture over the fillets, coating them evenly.
4. Bake in the preheated oven for 15-20 minutes, or until the fish is cooked through and flakes easily with a fork.
5. Serve hot with lemon wedges on the side.

Nutritional Information (per serving): Calories: 280 | Protein: 30g | Carbohydrates: 2g | Fats: 16g | Fiber: 0g | Cholesterol: 70mg | Sodium: 400mg

Health Benefits: This Herb-Crusted Sea Bass is rich in lean protein and healthy fats, promoting muscle health and heart wellness. The combination of fresh herbs, lemon, and olive oil provides essential nutrients and antioxidants, supporting overall health and aligning with the Mediterranean Diet's emphasis on fresh, nutritious ingredients.

Lemon Dill Scallops

Serves:4 | Prep Time:10 min | Cook Time:10 min

- 1 lb sea scallops, cleaned
- 3 tbsp olive oil
- 2 tbsp fresh lemon juice
- 1 tbsp lemon zest
- 3 cloves garlic, minced
- 2 tbsp fresh dill, chopped
- 1/2 tsp salt
- 1/4 tsp black pepper
- Fresh dill sprigs (for garnish)
- Lemon wedges (for serving)

1. Pat the scallops dry with paper towels and season with salt and pepper.
2. In a large skillet, heat 2 tablespoons of olive oil over medium-high heat. Add the scallops in a single layer and cook for 2-3 minutes per side, or until they are golden brown and opaque. Remove the scallops from the skillet and set aside.
3. In the same skillet, add the remaining tablespoon of olive oil, garlic, lemon juice, and lemon zest. Cook for about 1 minute until the garlic is fragrant.
4. Stir in the chopped dill and return the scallops to the skillet. Toss the scallops in the sauce until they are well coated and heated through.
5. Serve hot, garnished with fresh dill sprigs and lemon wedges on the side.

Nutritional Information (per serving): Calories: 250 | Protein: 20g | Carbohydrates: 3g | Fats: 16g | Fiber: 1g | Cholesterol: 60mg | Sodium: 400mg

Health Benefits: These Lemon Dill Scallops are rich in lean protein and healthy fats, supporting muscle health and overall wellness. The combination of fresh lemon and dill provides antioxidants and anti-inflammatory properties, aligning with the Mediterranean Diet's emphasis on fresh, nutritious ingredients.

Mediterranean Mussels in White Wine

Serves:4 | Prep Time:10 min | Cook Time:15 min

- 2 lbs fresh mussels, cleaned and debearded
- 2 tbsp olive oil
- 1 large onion, finely chopped
- 4 cloves garlic, minced
- 1 cup dry white wine
- 1 can (14 oz) diced tomatoes, drained
- 1 tsp dried oregano
- 1 tsp dried thyme
- 1/2 tsp red pepper flakes (optional)
- 1/2 tsp salt
- 1/4 tsp black pepper
- 1/4 cup fresh parsley, chopped
- Lemon wedges (for serving)
- Crusty bread (for serving, optional)

1. Heat the olive oil in a large pot over medium heat. Add the chopped onion and garlic, and sauté until softened.
2. Pour in the white wine and bring to a simmer. Let it cook for 2-3 minutes to reduce slightly.
3. Add the diced tomatoes, oregano, thyme, red pepper flakes (if using), salt, and black pepper. Stir well to combine and bring to a simmer.
4. Add the cleaned mussels to the pot, cover, and cook for 5-7 minutes, or until the mussels have opened. Discard any mussels that do not open.
5. Stir in the chopped parsley.
6. Serve the mussels hot, with lemon wedges on the side and crusty bread for dipping if desired.

Nutritional Information (per serving): Calories: 250 | Protein: 18g | Carbohydrates: 10g | Fats: 10g | Fiber: 2g | Cholesterol: 60mg | Sodium: 600mg

Health Benefits: These Mediterranean Mussels in White Wine are rich in lean protein and essential minerals, supporting muscle health and overall wellness. The combination of fresh herbs, tomatoes, and olive oil provides antioxidants and heart-healthy fats, aligning with the Mediterranean Diet's principles of using fresh, nutritious ingredients.

CHAPTER 7

VEGETABLES AND SIDES - COLORFUL AND NUTRITIOUS SIDE DISHES

Roasted Vegetable Medley

Serves:4 | Prep Time:10 min | Cook Time:30 min

- 1 red bell pepper, chopped
- 1 yellow bell pepper, chopped
- 1 zucchini, sliced
- 1 eggplant, chopped
- 1 red onion, chopped
- 2 cloves garlic, minced
- 3 tbsp olive oil
- 1 tsp dried oregano
- 1 tsp dried thyme
- 1/2 tsp salt
- 1/4 tsp black pepper
- Fresh basil, chopped (for garnish)
- Balsamic glaze (optional, for serving)

1. Preheat your oven to 425°F (220°C).
2. In a large bowl, combine the chopped red bell pepper, yellow bell pepper, zucchini, eggplant, and red onion.
3. Add the minced garlic, olive oil, oregano, thyme, salt, and black pepper. Toss to coat the vegetables evenly.
4. Spread the vegetables in a single layer on a large baking sheet.
5. Roast in the preheated oven for 25-30 minutes, or until the vegetables are tender and slightly caramelized, stirring halfway through cooking.
6. Remove from the oven and transfer to a serving dish. Garnish with fresh basil and drizzle with balsamic glaze if desired.

Nutritional Information (per serving): Calories: 150 | Protein: 2g | Carbohydrates: 12g | Fats: 10g | Fiber: 4g | Cholesterol: 0mg | Sodium: 300mg

Health Benefits: This Roasted Vegetable Medley is rich in fiber and essential vitamins, supporting digestive health and overall wellness. The combination of fresh vegetables and olive oil provides heart-healthy fats and antioxidants, aligning with the Mediterranean Diet's emphasis on fresh, nutritious ingredients.

Grilled Asparagus with Lemon

Serves:4 | Prep Time:5 min | Cook Time:10 min

- 1 lb asparagus, trimmed
- 2 tbsp olive oil
- 1 lemon (zest and juice)
- 2 cloves garlic, minced
- 1/2 tsp salt
- 1/4 tsp black pepper
- Fresh parsley, chopped (for garnish)

1. Preheat the grill or grill pan over medium-high heat.
2. In a large bowl, toss the asparagus with olive oil, minced garlic, lemon zest, salt, and black pepper.
3. Place the asparagus on the grill in a single layer. Grill for about 3-4 minutes per side, or until tender and slightly charred.
4. Remove from the grill and transfer to a serving plate. Squeeze fresh lemon juice over the top.
5. Garnish with chopped fresh parsley before serving.

Nutritional Information (per serving): Calories: 80 | Protein: 2g | Carbohydrates: 5g | Fats: 7g | Fiber: 2g | Cholesterol: 0mg | Sodium: 150mg

Health Benefits: This Grilled Asparagus with Lemon is low in calories and high in fiber, supporting digestive health and weight management. The fresh asparagus provides essential vitamins and minerals, while the olive oil and lemon add heart-healthy fats and antioxidants, aligning with the Mediterranean Diet's emphasis on fresh, nutritious ingredients.

Balsamic Glazed Brussels Sprouts

Serves:4 | Prep Time:10 min | Cook Time:20 min

- 1 lb Brussels sprouts, trimmed and halved
- 2 tbsp olive oil
- 3 tbsp balsamic vinegar
- 1 tbsp honey
- 2 cloves garlic, minced
- 1/2 tsp salt
- 1/4 tsp black pepper
- 1/4 cup chopped walnuts (optional)
- Fresh parsley, chopped (for garnish)

1. Preheat your oven to 400°F (200°C).
2. In a large bowl, toss the Brussels sprouts with olive oil, minced garlic, salt, and black pepper.
3. Spread the Brussels sprouts in a single layer on a baking sheet.
4. Roast in the preheated oven for 15-20 minutes, or until the Brussels sprouts are tender and caramelized, stirring halfway through.
5. While the Brussels sprouts are roasting, combine the balsamic vinegar and honey in a small saucepan. Bring to a simmer over medium heat and cook for about 5 minutes, or until the glaze has thickened slightly.
6. Remove the Brussels sprouts from the oven and drizzle with the balsamic glaze. Toss to coat evenly.
7. Optional: Sprinkle with chopped walnuts for added crunch.
8. Serve hot, garnished with fresh parsley.

Nutritional Information (per serving): Calories: 150 | Protein: 3g | Carbohydrates: 15g | Fats: 9g | Fiber: 4g | Cholesterol: 0mg | Sodium: 250mg

Health Benefits: These Balsamic Glazed Brussels Sprouts are rich in fiber and essential vitamins, supporting digestive health and overall wellness. The combination of Brussels sprouts, olive oil, and balsamic vinegar provides heart-healthy fats and antioxidants, aligning with the Mediterranean Diet's emphasis on fresh, nutritious ingredients.

Mediterranean Stuffed Zucchini

Serves:4 | Prep Time:15 min | Cook Time:30 min

- 4 medium zucchini, halved lengthwise
- 2 tbsp olive oil
- 1 small onion, finely chopped
- 2 cloves garlic, minced
- 1/2 lb lean ground turkey or beef
- 1 cup cooked quinoa
- 1 can (14 oz) diced tomatoes, drained
- 1/4 cup crumbled feta cheese
- 1/4 cup chopped kalamata olives
- 2 tbsp chopped fresh parsley
- 1 tsp dried oregano
- 1/2 tsp salt
- 1/4 tsp black pepper
- Fresh basil, chopped (for garnish)

1. Preheat your oven to 375°F (190°C).
2. Scoop out the center of each zucchini half to create a hollow space for the filling. Place the zucchini halves in a baking dish.
3. In a large skillet, heat the olive oil over medium heat. Add the chopped onion and garlic, and sauté until softened.
4. Add the ground turkey or beef to the skillet and cook until browned. Stir in the cooked quinoa, diced tomatoes, crumbled feta cheese, chopped olives, parsley, oregano, salt, and black pepper. Mix well to combine.
5. Spoon the filling into the hollowed zucchini halves, pressing it down gently to pack it in.
6. Cover the baking dish with foil and bake in the preheated oven for 20 minutes. Remove the foil and bake for an additional 10 minutes, or until the zucchini is tender and the filling is heated through.
7. Serve hot, garnished with fresh basil.

Nutritional Information (per serving): Calories: 250 | Protein: 18g | Carbohydrates: 20g | Fats: 12g | Fiber: 5g | Cholesterol: 40mg | Sodium: 450mg

Health Benefits: This Mediterranean Stuffed Zucchini is rich in protein and fiber, promoting muscle health and digestive wellness. The combination of lean meat, quinoa, and fresh vegetables provides essential nutrients and antioxidants, supporting overall health and aligning with the Mediterranean Diet's principles of using fresh, nutritious ingredients.

Spiced Roasted Carrots

Serves:4 | Prep Time:10 min | Cook Time:30 min

- 1 lb carrots, peeled and cut into sticks
- 2 tbsp olive oil
- 1 tsp ground cumin
- 1 tsp ground coriander
- 1/2 tsp smoked paprika
- 1/2 tsp ground cinnamon
- 1/2 tsp salt
- 1/4 tsp black pepper
- Fresh parsley, chopped (for garnish)
- Lemon wedges (for serving)

1. Preheat your oven to 400°F (200°C).
2. In a large bowl, toss the carrot sticks with olive oil, ground cumin, ground coriander, smoked paprika, ground cinnamon, salt, and black pepper until well coated.
3. Spread the carrots in a single layer on a baking sheet.
4. Roast in the preheated oven for 25-30 minutes, or until the carrots are tender and slightly caramelized, stirring halfway through.
5. Remove from the oven and transfer to a serving dish. Garnish with fresh parsley and serve with lemon wedges on the side.

Nutritional Information (per serving): Calories: 120 | Protein: 1g | Carbohydrates: 10g | Fats: 9g | Fiber: 3g | Cholesterol: 0mg | Sodium: 250mg

Health Benefits: These Spiced Roasted Carrots are rich in fiber and essential vitamins, supporting digestive health and overall wellness. The combination of spices and olive oil provides antioxidants and heart-healthy fats, aligning with the Mediterranean Diet's emphasis on fresh, nutritious ingredients.

Greek-Style Spinach Pie

Serves:6 | Prep Time:20 min | Cook Time:30 min

- 1 lb fresh spinach, washed and chopped
- 1 small onion, finely chopped
- 3 cloves garlic, minced
- 2 tbsp olive oil
- 1/2 cup crumbled feta cheese
- 1/4 cup grated Parmesan cheese
- 2 tbsp fresh dill, chopped
- 2 tbsp fresh parsley, chopped
- 3 eggs, lightly beaten
- 1/2 tsp salt
- 1/4 tsp black pepper
- 8 sheets phyllo dough, thawed
- Cooking spray or additional olive oil for brushing

1. Preheat your oven to 375°F (190°C).
2. In a large skillet, heat the olive oil over medium heat. Add the chopped onion and garlic, and sauté until softened.
3. Add the chopped spinach to the skillet and cook until wilted. Remove from heat and let cool slightly.
4. In a large bowl, combine the cooked spinach mixture, crumbled feta cheese, grated Parmesan cheese, chopped dill, parsley, beaten eggs, salt, and black pepper. Mix well.
5. Lightly spray or brush a baking dish with cooking spray or olive oil. Lay one sheet of phyllo dough in the dish, allowing the edges to hang over the sides. Brush with olive oil or spray lightly with cooking spray. Repeat with three more sheets, brushing each layer.
6. Spread the spinach mixture evenly over the phyllo layers in the dish.
7. Cover the spinach mixture with the remaining four sheets of phyllo dough, brushing each layer with olive oil or cooking spray. Fold the overhanging edges over the top to seal the pie.
8. Bake in the preheated oven for 25-30 minutes, or until the phyllo is golden brown and crispy.
9. Let the pie cool for a few minutes before slicing and serving.

Nutritional Information (per serving): Calories: 250 | Protein: 10g | Carbohydrates: 20g | Fats: 15g | Fiber: 3g | Cholesterol: 80mg | Sodium: 450mg

Health Benefits: This Greek-Style Spinach Pie is rich in vitamins, minerals, and fiber, supporting overall wellness and digestive health. The combination of spinach and fresh herbs provides antioxidants, while the use of olive oil and feta cheese offers heart-healthy fats, aligning with the Mediterranean Diet's emphasis on fresh, nutritious ingredients.

Lemon Garlic Green Beans

Serves:4 | Prep Time:10 min | Cook Time:10 min

- 1 lb green beans, trimmed
- 2 tbsp olive oil
- 3 cloves garlic, minced
- 1 tbsp fresh lemon juice
- 1 tsp lemon zest
- 1/2 tsp salt
- 1/4 tsp black pepper
- Fresh parsley, chopped (for garnish)

1. Bring a large pot of water to a boil. Add the green beans and cook for 3-4 minutes, or until they are tender-crisp. Drain and set aside.
2. In a large skillet, heat the olive oil over medium heat. Add the minced garlic and sauté for about 1 minute, or until fragrant.
3. Add the cooked green beans to the skillet and toss to coat in the garlic oil. Cook for another 2-3 minutes.
4. Remove from heat and stir in the fresh lemon juice and lemon zest. Season with salt and black pepper.
5. Serve hot, garnished with chopped fresh parsley.

Nutritional Information (per serving): Calories: 80 | Protein: 2g | Carbohydrates: 8g | Fats: 5g | Fiber: 3g | Cholesterol: 0mg | Sodium: 150mg

Health Benefits: These Lemon Garlic Green Beans are low in calories and high in fiber, supporting digestive health and weight management. The green beans provide essential vitamins and minerals, while the olive oil and garlic add heart-healthy fats and antioxidants, aligning with the Mediterranean Diet's emphasis on fresh, nutritious ingredients.

Marinated Artichoke Hearts

Serves:4 | Prep Time:10 min | Cook Time:5 min

- 1 can (14 oz) artichoke hearts, drained and rinsed
- 1/4 cup olive oil
- 2 tbsp fresh lemon juice
- 2 cloves garlic, minced
- 1 tsp dried oregano
- 1/2 tsp dried thyme
- 1/2 tsp salt
- 1/4 tsp black pepper
- 1/4 cup fresh parsley, chopped
- Lemon wedges (for serving)

1. In a large bowl, whisk together the olive oil, lemon juice, minced garlic, dried oregano, dried thyme, salt, and black pepper.
2. Add the drained artichoke hearts to the bowl and toss gently to coat them in the marinade.
3. Cover and refrigerate for at least 1 hour to allow the flavors to meld.

4. Before serving, let the artichokes sit at room temperature for about 10 minutes. Garnish with fresh parsley and serve with lemon wedges.

Nutritional Information (per serving): Calories: 140 | Protein: 2g | Carbohydrates: 6g | Fats: 12g | Fiber: 4g | Cholesterol: 0mg | Sodium: 300mg

Health Benefits: These Marinated Artichoke Hearts are rich in fiber and essential vitamins, supporting digestive health and overall wellness. The combination of artichokes, olive oil, and fresh herbs provides heart-healthy fats and antioxidants, aligning with the Mediterranean Diet's emphasis on fresh, nutritious ingredients.

Roasted Red Pepper Salad

Serves:4 | Prep Time:10 min | Cook Time:20 min

- 4 large red bell peppers
- 2 tbsp olive oil
- 1 tbsp red wine vinegar
- 2 cloves garlic, minced
- 1/2 tsp salt
- 1/4 tsp black pepper
- 1/4 cup fresh basil leaves, chopped
- 1/4 cup fresh parsley, chopped
- 1/4 cup crumbled feta cheese (optional)
- Lemon wedges (for serving)

1. Preheat your oven to 450°F (230°C).
2. Place the red bell peppers on a baking sheet and roast in the preheated oven for about 20 minutes, turning occasionally, until the skins are charred and blistered.
3. Remove the peppers from the oven and place them in a bowl. Cover with plastic wrap and let them steam for about 10 minutes. This will make the skins easier to peel off.
4. Once cooled, peel the skins off the peppers and remove the seeds. Slice the peppers into thin strips.
5. In a large bowl, whisk together the olive oil, red wine vinegar, minced garlic, salt, and black pepper.
6. Add the sliced peppers to the bowl and toss gently to coat them in the dressing.
7. Stir in the chopped basil and parsley.
8. Optional: Sprinkle with crumbled feta cheese for added flavor.
9. Serve at room temperature or chilled, with lemon wedges on the side.

Nutritional Information (per serving): Calories: 100 | Protein: 2g | Carbohydrates: 10g | Fats: 7g | Fiber: 3g | Cholesterol: 0mg | Sodium: 250mg

Health Benefits: This Roasted Red Pepper Salad is rich in vitamins A and C, supporting immune health and skin wellness.

Herb-Roasted Potatoes

Serves:4 | Prep Time:10 min | Cook Time:35 min

- 1 1/2 lbs baby potatoes, halved
- 3 tbsp olive oil
- 3 cloves garlic, minced
- 1 tsp dried rosemary
- 1 tsp dried thyme
- 1/2 tsp dried oregano
- 1/2 tsp salt
- 1/4 tsp black pepper
- Fresh parsley, chopped (for garnish)
- Lemon wedges (for serving)

1. Preheat your oven to 425°F (220°C).
2. In a large bowl, toss the halved baby potatoes with olive oil, minced garlic, dried rosemary, thyme, oregano, salt, and black pepper until evenly coated.
3. Spread the potatoes in a single layer on a baking sheet.
4. Roast in the preheated oven for 30-35 minutes, or until the potatoes are golden brown and crispy, stirring halfway through.
5. Remove from the oven and transfer to a serving dish. Garnish with fresh parsley and serve with lemon wedges on the side.

Nutritional Information (per serving): Calories: 200 | Protein: 3g | Carbohydrates: 28g | Fats: 9g | Fiber: 3g | Cholesterol: 0mg | Sodium: 300mg

Health Benefits: These Herb-Roasted Potatoes are a good source of complex carbohydrates and fiber, supporting digestive health and sustained energy levels. The combination of potatoes, olive oil, and herbs provides antioxidants and heart-healthy fats, aligning with the Mediterranean Diet's emphasis on fresh, nutritious ingredients.

Mediterranean Cabbage Rolls

Serves:4 | Prep Time:10 min | Cook Time:20 min

- 8 large cabbage leaves
- 1 lb ground turkey or beef
- 1/2 cup cooked quinoa (prepare in advance or use pre-cooked)
- 1 small onion, finely chopped
- 2 cloves garlic, minced
- 1 can (14 oz) diced tomatoes, drained
- 1/4 cup crumbled feta cheese
- 2 tbsp chopped fresh parsley
- 1 tsp dried oregano
- 1/2 tsp salt
- 1/4 tsp black pepper
- 1 cup tomato sauce

1. Preheat your oven to 375°F (190°C).
2. Bring a large pot of water to a boil, then blanch the cabbage leaves for 1-2 minutes until softened. Drain and set aside.

3. In a large bowl, mix the ground turkey or beef, cooked quinoa, onion, garlic, diced tomatoes, feta cheese, parsley, oregano, salt, and black pepper.

4. Place a portion of the filling in the center of each cabbage leaf and roll up, folding in the sides to enclose the filling.

5. Place the rolls seam-side down in a baking dish and pour the tomato sauce over them.

6. Cover and bake for 15-20 minutes, until the rolls are cooked through.

7. Serve hot.

Nutritional Information (per serving): Calories: 300 | Protein: 25g | Carbohydrates: 20g | Fats: 10g | Fiber: 5g | Cholesterol: 60mg | Sodium: 500mg

Health Benefits: Mediterranean Cabbage Rolls are high in protein and fiber, promoting muscle health and digestive wellness. The combination of lean meat, quinoa, and fresh vegetables provides essential nutrients and antioxidants, supporting overall health and aligning with the Mediterranean Diet's principles of fresh, nutritious ingredients.

Spicy Roasted Cauliflower

Serves:4 | Prep Time:10 min | Cook Time:25 min

- 1 large head cauliflower, cut into florets
- 2 tbsp olive oil
- 1 tsp smoked paprika
- 1/2 tsp ground cumin
- 1/2 tsp ground turmeric
- 1/4 tsp cayenne pepper (optional)
- 1/2 tsp salt
- 1/4 tsp black pepper
- Fresh cilantro, chopped (for garnish)
- Lemon wedges (for serving)

1. Preheat your oven to 425°F (220°C).

2. In a large bowl, toss the cauliflower florets with olive oil, smoked paprika, cumin, turmeric, cayenne pepper (if using), salt, and black pepper until well coated.

3. Spread the cauliflower in a single layer on a baking sheet.

4. Roast in the preheated oven for 20-25 minutes, stirring halfway through, until the cauliflower is tender and slightly crispy.

5. Remove from the oven and transfer to a serving dish. Garnish with fresh cilantro and serve with lemon wedges.

Nutritional Information (per serving): Calories: 120 | Protein: 3g | Carbohydrates: 10g | Fats: 8g | Fiber: 4g | Cholesterol: 0mg | Sodium: 250mg

Health Benefits: Spicy Roasted Cauliflower is low in calories and high in fiber, supporting digestive health and weight management.

Stuffed Portobello Mushrooms

Serves:4 | Prep Time:15 min | Cook Time:20 min

- 4 large portobello mushrooms, stems removed
- 2 tbsp olive oil
- 1 small onion, finely chopped
- 2 cloves garlic, minced
- 1/2 cup cooked quinoa
- 1/4 cup sun-dried tomatoes, chopped
- 1/4 cup crumbled feta cheese
- 2 tbsp chopped fresh basil
- 1 tsp dried oregano
- 1/2 tsp salt
- 1/4 tsp black pepper
- Balsamic glaze (optional, for serving)

1. Preheat your oven to 375°F (190°C).

2. In a large skillet, heat 1 tablespoon of olive oil over medium heat. Add the chopped onion and garlic, and sauté until softened.

3. Stir in the cooked quinoa, sun-dried tomatoes, feta cheese, basil, oregano, salt, and black pepper.

4. Brush the portobello mushrooms with the remaining olive oil and place them on a baking sheet.

5. Spoon the quinoa mixture into the mushroom caps.

6. Bake in the preheated oven for 15-20 minutes, until the mushrooms are tender.

7. Optional: Drizzle with balsamic glaze before serving.

Nutritional Information (per serving): Calories: 200 | Protein: 6g | Carbohydrates: 12g | Fats: 14g | Fiber: 3g | Cholesterol: 10mg | Sodium: 400mg

Health Benefits: Stuffed Portobello Mushrooms are rich in fiber and essential vitamins, supporting digestive health and overall wellness. The combination of quinoa, sun-dried tomatoes, and fresh herbs provides antioxidants and heart-healthy fats, aligning with the Mediterranean Diet's emphasis on fresh, nutritious ingredients.

Mediterranean Ratatouille

Serves:4 | Prep Time:15 min | Cook Time:30 min

- 1 eggplant, diced
- 1 zucchini, diced
- 1 red bell pepper, chopped
- 1 yellow bell pepper, chopped
- 1 red onion, chopped
- 3 cloves garlic, minced
- 3 tbsp olive oil
- 1 can (14 oz) diced tomatoes
- 1 tsp dried thyme
- 1 tsp dried oregano
- 1/2 tsp salt
- 1/4 tsp black pepper
- Fresh basil, chopped (for garnish)

1. Preheat your oven to 400°F (200°C).
2. In a large bowl, toss the eggplant, zucchini, red bell pepper, yellow bell pepper, red onion, and garlic with olive oil, thyme, oregano, salt, and black pepper.
3. Spread the vegetables in a single layer on a baking sheet.
4. Roast in the preheated oven for 20 minutes.
5. Remove from the oven, stir in the diced tomatoes, and return to the oven for an additional 10 minutes.
6. Transfer to a serving dish and garnish with fresh basil.

Nutritional Information (per serving): Calories: 180 | Protein: 3g | Carbohydrates: 20g | Fats: 10g | Fiber: 5g | Cholesterol: 0mg | Sodium: 300mg

Health Benefits: Mediterranean Ratatouille is rich in vitamins and antioxidants, promoting overall health and immune function. The combination of fresh vegetables and olive oil provides heart-healthy fats and essential nutrients, aligning with the Mediterranean Diet's principles of using fresh, nutritious ingredients.

Lemon and Dill Roasted Broccoli

Serves:4 | Prep Time:10 min | Cook Time:20 min

- 1 lb broccoli florets
- 2 tbsp olive oil
- 2 cloves garlic, minced
- 1 tbsp fresh lemon juice
- 1 tsp lemon zest
- 1 tbsp fresh dill, chopped
- 1/2 tsp salt
- 1/4 tsp black pepper

1. Preheat your oven to 425°F (220°C).
2. In a large bowl, toss the broccoli florets with olive oil, minced garlic, lemon juice, lemon zest, fresh dill, salt, and black pepper until well coated.
3. Spread the broccoli in a single layer on a baking sheet.
4. Roast in the preheated oven for 15-20 minutes, or until the broccoli is tender and slightly crispy, stirring halfway through.
5. Remove from the oven and transfer to a serving dish.

Nutritional Information (per serving): Calories: 90 | Protein: 3g | Carbohydrates: 8g | Fats: 6g | Fiber: 3g | Cholesterol: 0mg | Sodium: 200mg

Health Benefits: It is low in calories and high in fiber, supporting digestive health and weight management. The fresh broccoli provides essential vitamins and minerals, while the olive oil and dill add heart-healthy fats and antioxidants, aligning with the Mediterranean Diet's emphasis on fresh, nutritious ingredients.

CHAPTER 8

VEGETARIAN MAINS - SATISFYING MEATLESS MEALS

Eggplant Parmesan

Serves:4 | Prep Time:10 min | Cook Time:20 min

- 2 medium eggplants, sliced into 1/2-inch rounds
- 1/4 cup olive oil
- 2 cups marinara sauce
- 1 cup shredded mozzarella cheese
- 1/2 cup grated Parmesan cheese
- 1/2 cup whole wheat bread crumbs
- 1/4 cup fresh basil, chopped
- 1 tsp dried oregano
- 1/2 tsp salt
- 1/4 tsp black pepper

1. Preheat your oven to 375°F (190°C).
2. Brush the eggplant slices with olive oil and season with salt and pepper. Arrange them on a baking sheet and bake for 10 minutes, flipping halfway through.
3. In a baking dish, spread 1/2 cup of marinara sauce. Layer half of the baked eggplant slices over the sauce.
4. Top the eggplant with another 1/2 cup of marinara sauce, 1/2 cup of mozzarella cheese, and 1/4 cup of Parmesan cheese.
5. Repeat the layers with the remaining eggplant, marinara sauce, mozzarella cheese, and Parmesan cheese.
6. Sprinkle the bread crumbs and dried oregano on top.
7. Bake for an additional 10 minutes, or until the cheese is bubbly and golden.
8. Garnish with fresh basil before serving.

Nutritional Information (per serving): Calories: 320 | Protein: 14g | Carbohydrates: 24g | Fats: 20g | Fiber: 6g | Cholesterol: 30mg | Sodium: 600mg

Health Benefits: Eggplant Parmesan is rich in fiber and antioxidants, promoting digestive health and reducing inflammation. The combination of eggplant, marinara sauce, and cheese provides essential vitamins and minerals, aligning with the Mediterranean Diet's principles of fresh, nutritious ingredients.

Spinach and Feta Stuffed Peppers

Serves:4 | Prep Time:15 min | Cook Time:30 min

- 4 large bell peppers, tops cut off and seeds removed
- 1 tbsp olive oil
- 1 small onion, finely chopped
- 2 cloves garlic, minced
- 1 bag (10 oz) fresh spinach, chopped
- 1 cup cooked quinoa
- 1/2 cup crumbled feta cheese
- 1 tsp dried oregano
- 1/2 tsp salt
- 1/4 tsp black pepper
- Fresh parsley, chopped (for garnish)

1. Preheat your oven to 375°F (190°C).
2. In a large skillet, heat the olive oil over medium heat. Add the chopped onion and garlic, and sauté until softened.
3. Add the chopped spinach to the skillet and cook until wilted. Remove from heat and stir in the cooked quinoa, crumbled feta cheese, oregano, salt, and black pepper.
4. Stuff the bell peppers with the spinach and quinoa mixture, pressing down gently to pack it in.
5. Place the stuffed peppers in a baking dish and cover with foil.
6. Bake in the preheated oven for 20 minutes. Remove the foil and bake for an additional 10 minutes, or until the peppers are tender.
7. Garnish with fresh parsley before serving.

Nutritional Information (per serving): Calories: 220 | Protein: 8g | Carbohydrates: 25g | Fats: 10g | Fiber: 6g | Cholesterol: 20mg | Sodium: 400mg

Health Benefits: Spinach and Feta Stuffed Peppers are high in fiber and essential vitamins, supporting digestive health and overall wellness. The combination of spinach, quinoa, and feta provides antioxidants and heart-healthy fats, aligning with the Mediterranean Diet's emphasis on fresh, nutritious ingredients.

Mediterranean Veggie Stir-Fry

Serves:4 | Prep Time:15 min | Cook Time:15 min

- 2 tbsp olive oil
- 1 red onion, sliced
- 2 cloves garlic, minced
- 1 red bell pepper, sliced
- 1 yellow bell pepper, sliced
- 1 zucchini, sliced
- 1 cup cherry tomatoes, halved
- 1/4 cup Kalamata olives, pitted and halved
- 1 tsp dried oregano
- 1/2 tsp salt
- 1/4 tsp black pepper
- Fresh basil, chopped (for garnish)

1. In a large skillet or wok, heat the olive oil over medium-high heat. Add the sliced red onion and garlic, and sauté for 2-3 minutes.
2. Add the sliced red bell pepper, yellow bell pepper, and zucchini. Stir-fry for 5-7 minutes, or until the vegetables are tender-crisp.
3. Stir in the cherry tomatoes, Kalamata olives, oregano, salt, and black pepper. Cook for an additional 2-3 minutes, until the tomatoes are softened.
4. Remove from heat and transfer to a serving dish. Garnish with fresh basil before serving.

Nutritional Information (per serving): Calories: 180 | Protein: 3g | Carbohydrates: 14g | Fats: 12g | Fiber: 5g | Cholesterol: 0mg | Sodium: 350mg

Health Benefits: Mediterranean Veggie Stir-Fry is low in calories and rich in vitamins and antioxidants, promoting overall health and immune function. The combination of fresh vegetables and olive oil provides heart-healthy fats and essential nutrients, aligning with the Mediterranean Diet's principles of using fresh, nutritious ingredients.

Chickpea and Spinach Curry

Serves:4 | Prep Time:15 min | Cook Time:20 min

- 2 tbsp olive oil
- 1 large onion, chopped
- 3 cloves garlic, minced
- 1 tbsp fresh ginger, grated
- 1 tsp ground cumin
- 1 tsp ground coriander
- 1/2 tsp ground turmeric
- 1/4 tsp cayenne pepper (optional)
- 1 can (14 oz) diced tomatoes
- 1 can (14 oz) coconut milk
- 1 can (14 oz) chickpeas, drained and rinsed
- 1 bag (10 oz) fresh spinach, chopped
- 1 tsp salt
- 1/4 tsp black pepper
- Fresh cilantro, chopped (for garnish)
- Cooked rice or naan bread (for serving)

1. In a large pot, heat the olive oil over medium heat. Add the chopped onion, garlic, and ginger, and sauté until softened.
2. Stir in the ground cumin, coriander, turmeric, and cayenne pepper (if using). Cook for 1-2 minutes until fragrant.
3. Add the diced tomatoes, coconut milk, and chickpeas. Bring to a simmer and cook for 10 minutes, allowing the flavors to meld.
4. Stir in the chopped spinach, salt, and black pepper. Cook for an additional 5 minutes, or until the spinach is wilted.
5. Serve hot, garnished with fresh cilantro, and accompanied by cooked rice or naan bread.

Nutritional Information (per serving): Calories: 300 | Protein: 8g | Carbohydrates: 25g | Fats: 18g | Fiber: 6g | Cholesterol: 0mg | Sodium: 500mg

Health Benefits: Chickpea and Spinach Curry is rich in fiber and plant-based protein, promoting digestive health and muscle wellness. The combination of chickpeas, spinach, and spices provides essential vitamins, minerals, and antioxidants, aligning with the Mediterranean Diet's emphasis on fresh, nutritious ingredients.

Zucchini Noodles with Pesto

Serves:4 | Prep Time:15 min | Cook Time:5 min

- 4 medium zucchini, spiralized into noodles
- 2 cups fresh basil leaves
- 1/4 cup pine nuts
- 2 cloves garlic
- 1/2 cup grated Parmesan cheese
- 1/2 cup olive oil
- 1/2 tsp salt
- 1/4 tsp black pepper
- Cherry tomatoes, halved (optional, for garnish)

1. In a food processor, combine the basil leaves, pine nuts, garlic, Parmesan cheese, salt, and black pepper. Pulse until the ingredients are finely chopped.
2. With the food processor running, slowly add the olive oil until the mixture is smooth and creamy.
3. In a large skillet, heat a small amount of olive oil over medium heat. Add the zucchini noodles and sauté for 2-3 minutes until just tender.
4. Remove from heat and toss the zucchini noodles with the prepared pesto sauce.
5. Serve immediately, garnished with cherry tomatoes if desired.

Nutritional Information (per serving): Calories: 300 | Protein: 6g | Carbohydrates: 8g | Fats: 28g | Fiber: 3g | Cholesterol: 10mg | Sodium: 300mg

Health Benefits: Zucchini Noodles with Pesto are low in carbohydrates and calories, supporting weight management and digestive health. The fresh basil and olive oil provide heart-healthy fats and antioxidants, aligning with the Mediterranean Diet's principles of fresh, nutritious ingredients.

Stuffed Acorn Squash

Serves:4 | Prep Time:10 min | Cook Time:20 min

- 2 acorn squash, halved and seeds removed
- 1 tbsp olive oil
- 1 small onion, chopped
- 2 cloves garlic, minced
- 1/2 lb ground turkey or beef
- 1 cup cooked quinoa (use pre-cooked or microwaveable for convenience)
- 1/4 cup dried cranberries
- 1/4 cup chopped walnuts
- 1 tsp dried thyme
- 1/2 tsp ground cinnamon
- 1/2 tsp salt
- 1/4 tsp black pepper
- Fresh parsley, chopped (for garnish)

1. Pre-cook the Squash: Preheat your oven to 425°F (220°C). Place the acorn squash halves cut-side down on a microwave-safe plate with a bit of water. Microwave on high for 8-10 minutes until tender. Alternatively, if you prefer using the oven, you can roast them in the preheated oven for about 20 minutes.
2. Prepare the Filling: While the squash is cooking, heat the olive oil in a large skillet over medium heat. Add the chopped onion and garlic, and sauté until softened, about 3 minutes.
3. Cook the Meat: Add the ground turkey or beef to the skillet and cook until browned, about 5 minutes.
4. Combine Ingredients: Stir in the cooked quinoa, dried cranberries, chopped walnuts, thyme, cinnamon, salt, and black pepper. Cook for an additional 2-3 minutes, stirring to combine.
5. Stuff the Squash: Once the squash is tender, remove from the microwave or oven and place cut-side up on a baking sheet. Spoon the filling into each squash half, pressing down gently to pack it in.
6. Final Bake: If using the microwave method for pre-cooking the squash, bake the stuffed squash in the preheated oven for about 10 minutes to heat through and allow flavors to meld. If you roasted the squash, this step can be reduced to just a few minutes to melt the filling together.
7. Serve: Garnish with fresh parsley before serving.

Nutritional Information (per serving): Calories: 350 | Protein: 14g | Carbohydrates: 45g | Fats: 15g | Fiber: 7g | Cholesterol: 40mg | Sodium: 400mg

Health Benefits: Stuffed Acorn Squash is rich in fiber and essential vitamins, supporting digestive health and overall wellness. The combination of quinoa, dried cranberries, and walnuts provides antioxidants and heart-healthy fats, aligning with the Mediterranean Diet's emphasis on fresh, nutritious ingredients.

By microwaving the squash and using pre-cooked quinoa, you can significantly cut down on cooking time while still enjoying a delicious and nutritious meal.

Greek-Style Lentil Moussaka

Serves:4 | Prep Time:10 min | Cook Time:20 min

- 1 cup pre-cooked lentils (available canned or pre-cooked from the store)
- 1 eggplant, sliced into rounds
- 2 tbsp olive oil
- 1 onion, chopped
- 2 cloves garlic, minced
- 1 can (14 oz) diced tomatoes
- 1 tsp dried oregano
- 1/2 tsp ground cinnamon
- 1/2 tsp salt
- 1/4 tsp black pepper
- 1/2 cup crumbled feta cheese
- Fresh parsley, chopped (for garnish)

1. Preheat your oven to 425°F (220°C). This higher temperature will help speed up the cooking process.
2. In a large skillet, heat 1 tablespoon of olive oil over medium-high heat. Add the eggplant slices and cook until browned on both sides, about 3-4 minutes per side. Remove from the skillet and set aside.
3. In the same skillet, add the remaining olive oil, chopped onion, and garlic. Sauté until softened, about 3 minutes.
4. Stir in the diced tomatoes, pre-cooked lentils, oregano, cinnamon, salt, and black pepper. Cook for 5 minutes, allowing the flavors to meld.
5. In a baking dish, layer half of the eggplant slices, then spread the lentil mixture over them. Top with the remaining eggplant slices.
6. Sprinkle the crumbled feta cheese over the top.
7. Bake in the preheated oven for 10 minutes, or until the cheese is melted and golden.
8. Garnish with fresh parsley before serving.

Nutritional Information (per serving): Calories: 300 | Protein: 12g | Carbohydrates: 35g | Fats: 14g | Fiber: 10g | Cholesterol: 20mg | Sodium: 450mg

Health Benefits: It is high in fiber and plant-based protein, promoting digestive health and muscle wellness. The combination of lentils, eggplant, and tomatoes provides essential vitamins, minerals, and antioxidants, aligning with the Mediterranean Diet's emphasis on fresh, nutritious ingredients.

Spicy Chickpea and Tomato Stew

Serves:4 | Prep Time:10 min | Cook Time:30 min

- 2 tbsp olive oil
- 1 large onion, chopped
- 3 cloves garlic, minced
- 1 red chili, finely chopped (adjust to taste)
- 1 tsp ground cumin
- 1 tsp smoked paprika
- 1/2 tsp ground coriander
- 1/2 tsp ground turmeric
- 1 can (14 oz) diced tomatoes
- 1 can (14 oz) chickpeas, drained and rinsed
- 1 cup vegetable broth
- 1 bag (10 oz) fresh spinach, chopped
- 1 tsp salt
- 1/4 tsp black pepper
- Fresh cilantro, chopped (for garnish)

1. In a large pot, heat the olive oil over medium heat. Add the chopped onion, garlic, and red chili, and sauté until softened.
2. Stir in the ground cumin, smoked paprika, ground coriander, and ground turmeric. Cook for 1-2 minutes until fragrant.
3. Add the diced tomatoes, chickpeas, and vegetable broth. Bring to a simmer and cook for 15 minutes.
4. Stir in the chopped spinach, salt, and black pepper. Cook for an additional 5 minutes, or until the spinach is wilted.
5. Serve hot, garnished with fresh cilantro.

Nutritional Information (per serving): Calories: 250 | Protein: 8g | Carbohydrates: 30g | Fats: 10g | Fiber: 8g | Cholesterol: 0mg | Sodium: 500mg

Health Benefits: Spicy Chickpea and Tomato Stew is rich in fiber and plant-based protein, promoting digestive health and muscle wellness. The combination of chickpeas, spinach, and spices provides essential vitamins, minerals, and antioxidants, aligning with the Mediterranean Diet's emphasis on fresh, nutritious ingredients.

Cauliflower Rice Pilaf

Serves:4 | Prep Time:10 min | Cook Time:15 min

- 1 large head cauliflower, riced
- 2 tbsp olive oil
- 1 small onion, finely chopped
- 2 cloves garlic, minced
- 1 red bell pepper, chopped
- 1/4 cup sliced almonds
- 1/4 cup raisins
- 1 tsp ground cumin
- 1/2 tsp ground turmeric
- 1/2 tsp salt
- 1/4 tsp black pepper
- Fresh parsley, chopped (for garnish)

1. In a large skillet, heat the olive oil over medium heat. Add the onion and garlic, and sauté until softened, about 3 minutes.
2. Stir in the chopped red bell pepper, cumin, and turmeric. Cook for another 2 minutes.
3. Add the riced cauliflower and cook, stirring occasionally, for 5-7 minutes until tender.
4. Stir in the sliced almonds and raisins. Season with salt and black pepper.
5. Garnish with fresh parsley before serving.

Nutritional Information (per serving): Calories: 150 | Protein: 4g | Carbohydrates: 12g | Fats: 10g | Fiber: 4g | Cholesterol: 0mg | Sodium: 250mg

Health Benefits: Cauliflower Rice Pilaf is low in carbohydrates and rich in fiber, supporting digestive health and weight management. The combination of cauliflower, almonds, and spices provides essential nutrients and antioxidants, aligning with the Mediterranean Diet's emphasis on fresh, nutritious ingredients.

Mediterranean Vegetable Paella

Serves:4 | Prep Time:10 min | Cook Time:20 min

- 2 tbsp olive oil
- 1 small onion, finely chopped
- 3 cloves garlic, minced
- 1 red bell pepper, chopped
- 1 yellow bell pepper, chopped
- 1 zucchini, diced
- 1 cup Arborio rice
- 1 can (14 oz) diced tomatoes
- 2 cups vegetable broth
- 1 tsp smoked paprika
- 1/2 tsp saffron threads (optional)
- 1/2 tsp salt
- 1/4 tsp black pepper
- 1 cup frozen peas
- Fresh parsley, chopped (for garnish)

1. In a large skillet or paella pan, heat the olive oil over medium heat. Add the onion and garlic, and sauté until softened, about 3 minutes.
2. Stir in the chopped red and yellow bell peppers and zucchini. Cook for another 5 minutes.
3. Add the Arborio rice and cook, stirring, for 2 minutes.
4. Stir in the diced tomatoes, vegetable broth, smoked paprika, saffron (if using), salt, and black pepper. Bring to a boil.
5. Reduce heat to low and simmer, uncovered, for 15 minutes, stirring occasionally.
6. Stir in the frozen peas and cook for another 5 minutes, until the rice is tender.
7. Garnish with fresh parsley before serving.

Nutritional Information (per serving): Calories: 300 | Protein: 6g | Carbohydrates: 55g |

- Fats: 8g | Fiber: 6g | Cholesterol: 0mg | Sodium: 600mg

Health Benefits: Mediterranean Vegetable Paella is rich in fiber and antioxidants, promoting overall health and immune function. The combination of fresh vegetables and Arborio rice provides essential vitamins and minerals, aligning with the Mediterranean Diet's principles of fresh, nutritious ingredients.

Mushroom and Spinach Lasagna

Serves:4 | Prep Time:15 min | Cook Time:15 min

- 8 lasagna noodles, cooked according to package instructions
- 2 tbsp olive oil
- 2 cloves garlic, minced
- 1 small onion, chopped
- 1 lb mushrooms, sliced
- 1 bag (10 oz) fresh spinach, chopped
- 1 cup ricotta cheese
- 1 cup marinara sauce
- 1/2 cup shredded mozzarella cheese
- 1/4 cup grated Parmesan cheese
- 1 tsp dried oregano
- 1/2 tsp salt
- 1/4 tsp black pepper

1. Preheat your oven to 375°F (190°C).
2. In a large skillet, heat the olive oil over medium heat. Add the garlic and onion, and sauté until softened.
3. Add the mushrooms and cook until browned, about 5 minutes. Stir in the spinach and cook until wilted. Season with salt and black pepper.
4. In a baking dish, spread a thin layer of marinara sauce. Layer with lasagna noodles, ricotta cheese, mushroom-spinach mixture, and marinara sauce. Repeat layers.
5. Top with mozzarella cheese and Parmesan cheese. Sprinkle with dried oregano.
6. Bake in the preheated oven for 15 minutes, or until the cheese is melted and bubbly.

Nutritional Information (per serving): Calories: 400 | Protein: 20g | Carbohydrates: 45g | Fats: 18g | Fiber: 6g | Cholesterol: 50mg | Sodium: 700mg

Health Benefits: Mushroom and Spinach Lasagna is high in protein and fiber, promoting muscle health and digestive wellness. The combination of mushrooms, spinach, and cheeses provides essential vitamins, minerals, and antioxidants, aligning with the Mediterranean Diet's emphasis on fresh, nutritious ingredients.

Quinoa and Black Bean Stuffed Peppers

Serves:4 | Prep Time:10 min | Cook Time:20 min

- 4 large bell peppers, tops cut off and seeds removed
- 1 tbsp olive oil
- 1 small onion, chopped
- 2 cloves garlic, minced
- 1 cup cooked quinoa (use pre-cooked or microwaveable for convenience)
- 1 can (14 oz) black beans, drained and rinsed
- 1 cup corn kernels
- 1 tsp ground cumin
- 1/2 tsp chili powder
- 1/2 tsp salt
- 1/4 tsp black pepper
- 1/2 cup shredded cheddar cheese
- Fresh cilantro, chopped (for garnish)

1. Preheat your oven to 375°F (190°C).
2. In a large skillet, heat the olive oil over medium heat. Add the chopped onion and garlic, and sauté until softened, about 3 minutes.
3. Stir in the cooked quinoa, black beans, corn, cumin, chili powder, salt, and black pepper. Cook for 5 minutes, stirring to combine.
4. Stuff the bell peppers with the quinoa mixture, pressing down gently to pack it in.
5. Place the stuffed peppers in a baking dish and cover with foil.
6. Bake in the preheated oven for 15 minutes. Remove the foil, sprinkle with shredded cheddar cheese, and bake for an additional 5 minutes, until the cheese is melted.
7. Garnish with fresh cilantro before serving.

Nutritional Information (per serving): Calories: 300 | Protein: 12g | Carbohydrates: 45g | Fats: 10g | Fiber: 10g | Cholesterol: 10mg | Sodium: 400mg

Health Benefits: Quinoa and Black Bean Stuffed Peppers are rich in fiber and plant-based protein, promoting digestive health and muscle wellness. The combination of quinoa, black beans, and vegetables provides essential vitamins, minerals, and antioxidants, aligning with the Mediterranean Diet's emphasis on fresh, nutritious ingredients.

Greek-Style Veggie Skewers

Serves:4 | Prep Time:10 min | Cook Time:15 min

- 1 red bell pepper, chopped
- 1 yellow bell pepper, chopped
- 1 zucchini, sliced
- 1 red onion, chopped
- 1 cup cherry tomatoes
- 2 tbsp olive oil
- 1 tbsp lemon juice

- 1 tsp dried oregano
- 1/2 tsp garlic powder
- 1/2 tsp salt
- 1/4 tsp black pepper
- Wooden or metal skewers

1. Preheat your grill or grill pan over medium-high heat.
2. In a large bowl, combine the chopped bell peppers, zucchini, red onion, and cherry tomatoes.
3. In a small bowl, whisk together the olive oil, lemon juice, dried oregano, garlic powder, salt, and black pepper.
4. Pour the marinade over the vegetables and toss to coat.
5. Thread the vegetables onto skewers.
6. Grill the skewers for 10-15 minutes, turning occasionally, until the vegetables are tender and slightly charred.
7. Serve hot.

Nutritional Information (per serving): Calories: 150 | Protein: 3g | Carbohydrates: 15g | Fats: 10g | Fiber: 4g | Cholesterol: 0mg | Sodium: 200mg

Health Benefits: The combination of fresh vegetables and olive oil provides heart-healthy fats and essential nutrients, aligning with the Mediterranean Diet's principles of fresh, nutritious ingredients.

Spaghetti Squash Primavera

Serves:4 | Prep Time:10 min | Cook Time:20 min

- 1 large spaghetti squash
- 2 tbsp olive oil
- 2 cloves garlic, minced
- 1 small onion, chopped
- 1 red bell pepper, chopped
- 1 zucchini, diced
- 1 cup cherry tomatoes, halved
- 1/4 cup grated Parmesan cheese
- 1 tsp dried basil
- 1/2 tsp salt
- 1/4 tsp black pepper
- Fresh basil, chopped (for garnish)

1. Preheat your oven to 400°F (200°C).
2. Cut the spaghetti squash in half lengthwise and remove the seeds. Place cut-side down on a microwave-safe plate with a bit of water and microwave on high for 8-10 minutes until tender. Alternatively, roast in the preheated oven for about 20 minutes.
3. Using a fork, scrape the flesh of the squash to create spaghetti-like strands.
4. In a large skillet, heat the olive oil over medium heat. Add the garlic and onion, and sauté until softened, about 3 minutes.
5. Stir in the chopped red bell pepper, zucchini, and cherry tomatoes. Cook for another 5 minutes.

6. Add the spaghetti squash strands to the skillet and toss to combine.
7. Stir in the grated Parmesan cheese, dried basil, salt, and black pepper.
8. Serve hot, garnished with fresh basil.

Nutritional Information (per serving):
Calories: 200 | Protein: 6g | Carbohydrates: 25g | Fats: 10g | Fiber: 5g | Cholesterol: 10mg | Sodium: 300mg

Health Benefits: Spaghetti Squash Primavera is low in calories and high in fiber, supporting digestive health and weight management.

Lentil and Vegetable Shepherd's Pie

Serves:4 | Prep Time:15 min | Cook Time:25 min

- 2 tbsp olive oil
- 1 small onion, chopped
- 2 cloves garlic, minced
- 1 carrot, diced
- 1 cup cooked lentils (use pre-cooked or microwaveable for convenience)
- 1 cup frozen peas
- 1 cup corn kernels
- 1 tsp dried thyme
- 1/2 tsp dried rosemary
- 1/2 tsp salt
- 1/4 tsp black pepper
- 2 cups mashed potatoes (use pre-made or microwaveable for convenience)
- 1/4 cup grated Parmesan cheese
- Fresh parsley, chopped (for garnish)

1. Preheat your oven to 400°F (200°C).
2. In a large skillet, heat the olive oil over medium heat. Add the chopped onion, garlic, and diced carrot. Sauté until softened, about 5 minutes.
3. Stir in the cooked lentils, frozen peas, corn, thyme, rosemary, salt, and black pepper. Cook for another 5 minutes.
4. Transfer the lentil and vegetable mixture to a baking dish. Spread the mashed potatoes evenly over the top.
5. Sprinkle the grated Parmesan cheese over the mashed potatoes.
6. Bake in the preheated oven for 15 minutes, or until the top is golden brown.
7. Garnish with fresh parsley before serving.

Nutritional Information (per serving): Calories: 350 | Protein: 12g | Carbohydrates: 45g | Fats: 14g | Fiber: 10g | Cholesterol: 20mg | Sodium: 500mg

Health Benefits: Lentil and Vegetable Shepherd's Pie is rich in fiber and plant-based protein, promoting digestive health and muscle wellness.

CHAPTER 9

SALADS - CRISP AND REFRESHING SALADS

Greek Salad with Feta

Serves:4 | Prep Time:10 min | Cook Time:0 min

- 1 large cucumber, diced
- 1 pint cherry tomatoes, halved
- 1 red bell pepper, chopped
- 1 green bell pepper, chopped
- 1/2 red onion, thinly sliced
- 1/2 cup Kalamata olives, pitted
- 1/4 cup extra-virgin olive oil
- 2 tbsp red wine vinegar
- 1 tsp dried oregano
- 1/2 tsp salt
- 1/4 tsp black pepper
- 1/2 cup crumbled feta cheese
- Fresh parsley, chopped (for garnish)

1. In a large bowl, combine the cucumber, cherry tomatoes, red bell pepper, green bell pepper, red onion, and Kalamata olives.
2. In a small bowl, whisk together the olive oil, red wine vinegar, dried oregano, salt, and black pepper.
3. Pour the dressing over the salad and toss to combine.
4. Sprinkle the crumbled feta cheese over the top.
5. Garnish with fresh parsley before serving.

Nutritional Information (per serving): Calories: 200 | Protein: 4g | Carbohydrates: 10g | Fats: 16g | Fiber: 3g | Cholesterol: 15mg | Sodium: 400mg

Health Benefits: Greek Salad with Feta is rich in vitamins and antioxidants, promoting overall health and immune function. The combination of fresh vegetables, olive oil, and feta provides heart-healthy fats and essential nutrients, aligning with the Mediterranean Diet's principles of fresh, nutritious ingredients.

Mediterranean Quinoa Salad

Serves:4 | Prep Time:15 min | Cook Time:15 min

- 1 cup quinoa, rinsed
- 2 cups water
- 1 cucumber, diced
- 1 pint cherry tomatoes, halved
- 1 red bell pepper, chopped
- 1/2 red onion, finely chopped
- 1/4 cup Kalamata olives, pitted and halved
- 1/4 cup crumbled feta cheese
- 1/4 cup extra-virgin olive oil
- 2 tbsp lemon juice
- 1 tsp dried oregano
- 1/2 tsp salt
- 1/4 tsp black pepper
- Fresh mint, chopped (for garnish)

1. In a medium pot, bring the water to a boil. Add the quinoa, reduce the heat to low, cover, and simmer for 15 minutes, or until the quinoa is tender and the water is absorbed. Fluff with a fork and let cool.
2. In a large bowl, combine the cooled quinoa, cucumber, cherry tomatoes, red bell pepper, red onion, Kalamata olives, and crumbled feta cheese.
3. In a small bowl, whisk together the olive oil, lemon juice, dried oregano, salt, and black pepper.
4. Pour the dressing over the salad and toss to combine.
5. Garnish with fresh mint before serving.

Nutritional Information (per serving): Calories: 250 | Protein: 7g | Carbohydrates: 25g | Fats: 14g | Fiber: 5g | Cholesterol: 15mg | Sodium: 350mg

Health Benefits: Mediterranean Quinoa Salad is high in fiber and plant-based protein, promoting digestive health and muscle wellness. The combination of quinoa, fresh vegetables, and olive oil provides essential vitamins, minerals, and antioxidants, aligning with the Mediterranean Diet's emphasis on fresh, nutritious ingredients.

Chickpea and Cucumber Salad

Serves:4 | Prep Time:10 min | Cook Time:0 min

- 1 can (14 oz) chickpeas, drained and rinsed
- 1 large cucumber, diced
- 1 pint cherry tomatoes, halved
- 1/2 red onion, finely chopped
- 1/4 cup fresh parsley, chopped
- 1/4 cup extra-virgin olive oil
- 2 tbsp lemon juice
- 1 tsp ground cumin
- 1/2 tsp salt

- 1/4 tsp black pepper
- Crumbled feta cheese (optional, for garnish)

1. In a large bowl, combine the chickpeas, cucumber, cherry tomatoes, red onion, and fresh parsley.
2. In a small bowl, whisk together the olive oil, lemon juice, ground cumin, salt, and black pepper.
3. Pour the dressing over the salad and toss to combine.
4. Optional: Garnish with crumbled feta cheese before serving.

Nutritional Information (per serving): Calories: 200 | Protein: 5g | Carbohydrates: 20g | Fats: 12g | Fiber: 5g | Cholesterol: 0mg | Sodium: 250mg

Health Benefits: Chickpea and Cucumber Salad is rich in fiber and plant-based protein, promoting digestive health and muscle wellness. The combination of chickpeas, fresh vegetables, and olive oil provides essential vitamins, minerals, and antioxidants, aligning with the Mediterranean Diet's emphasis on fresh, nutritious ingredients.

Lemon Herb Tabbouleh

Serves:4 | Prep Time:15 min | Cook Time:15 min

- 1 cup bulgur wheat
- 2 cups water
- 1 large cucumber, diced
- 1 pint cherry tomatoes, halved
- 1/2 red onion, finely chopped
- 1 cup fresh parsley, chopped
- 1/4 cup fresh mint, chopped
- 1/4 cup fresh lemon juice
- 1/4 cup extra-virgin olive oil
- 1 tsp salt
- 1/4 tsp black pepper

1. In a medium pot, bring the water to a boil. Add the bulgur wheat, remove from heat, cover, and let sit for 15 minutes, or until the water is absorbed. Fluff with a fork and let cool.
2. In a large bowl, combine the cooled bulgur wheat, cucumber, cherry tomatoes, red onion, parsley, and mint.
3. In a small bowl, whisk together the lemon juice, olive oil, salt, and black pepper.
4. Pour the dressing over the salad and toss to combine.

Nutritional Information (per serving): Calories: 200 | Protein: 4g | Carbohydrates: 30g | Fats: 10g | Fiber: 6g | Cholesterol: 0mg | Sodium: 250mg

Health Benefits: The combination of bulgur wheat, fresh vegetables, and herbs provides essential vitamins and minerals, aligning with the Mediterranean Diet's principles of fresh, nutritious ingredients.

Spinach and Strawberry Salad

Serves:4 | Prep Time:10 min | Cook Time:0 min

- 6 cups baby spinach leaves
- 1 pint strawberries, hulled and sliced
- 1/4 red onion, thinly sliced
- 1/4 cup sliced almonds
- 1/4 cup crumbled feta cheese
- 1/4 cup balsamic vinaigrette

1. In a large bowl, combine the baby spinach, sliced strawberries, red onion, and sliced almonds.
2. Drizzle the balsamic vinaigrette over the salad and toss to combine.
3. Sprinkle with crumbled feta cheese before serving.

Nutritional Information (per serving): Calories: 180 | Protein: 4g | Carbohydrates: 15g | Fats: 12g | Fiber: 4g | Cholesterol: 10mg | Sodium: 200mg

Health Benefits: Spinach and Strawberry Salad is rich in vitamins and antioxidants, supporting immune function and overall health. The combination of spinach, strawberries, and almonds provides essential nutrients and heart-healthy fats, aligning with the Mediterranean Diet's emphasis on fresh, nutritious ingredients.

Roasted Beet and Goat Cheese Salad

Serves:4 | Prep Time:10 min | Cook Time:20 min

- 4 medium beets, peeled and diced
- 2 tbsp olive oil
- 6 cups mixed greens (such as arugula, spinach, and romaine)
- 1/4 red onion, thinly sliced
- 1/4 cup chopped walnuts
- 1/4 cup crumbled goat cheese
- 1/4 cup balsamic vinaigrette

1. Preheat your oven to 400°F (200°C).
2. Toss the diced beets with olive oil and spread them on a baking sheet. Roast in the preheated oven for 20 minutes, or until tender.
3. In a large bowl, combine the mixed greens, roasted beets, red onion, and walnuts.
4. Drizzle the balsamic vinaigrette over the salad and toss to combine.
5. Sprinkle with crumbled goat cheese before serving.

Nutritional Information (per serving): Calories: 220 | Protein: 6g | Carbohydrates: 18g | Fats: 16g | Fiber: 4g | Cholesterol: 10mg | Sodium: 200mg

Health Benefits: It is high in fiber and antioxidants, promoting digestive health and reducing inflammation. The combination of beets, mixed greens, and goat cheese provides essential vitamins and minerals.

Mediterranean Orzo Salad

Serves:4 | Prep Time:10 min | Cook Time:10 min

- 1 cup orzo pasta
- 1 pint cherry tomatoes, halved
- 1 cucumber, diced
- 1/2 red onion, finely chopped
- 1/4 cup Kalamata olives, pitted and halved
- 1/4 cup crumbled feta cheese
- 1/4 cup fresh parsley, chopped
- 1/4 cup extra-virgin olive oil
- 2 tbsp red wine vinegar
- 1 tsp dried oregano
- 1/2 tsp salt
- 1/4 tsp black pepper

1. Cook the orzo pasta according to package instructions. Drain and let cool.
2. In a large bowl, combine the cooled orzo, cherry tomatoes, cucumber, red onion, Kalamata olives, feta cheese, and parsley.
3. In a small bowl, whisk together the olive oil, red wine vinegar, dried oregano, salt, and black pepper.
4. Pour the dressing over the salad and toss to combine.

Nutritional Information (per serving): Calories: 300 | Protein: 7g | Carbohydrates: 35g | Fats: 14g | Fiber: 5g | Cholesterol: 10mg | Sodium: 400mg

Health Benefits: Mediterranean Orzo Salad is rich in fiber and antioxidants, promoting overall health and immune function. The combination of orzo, fresh vegetables, and olive oil provides essential vitamins and minerals, aligning with the Mediterranean Diet's principles of fresh, nutritious ingredients.

Tomato and Avocado Salad

Serves:4 | Prep Time:10 min | Cook Time:0 min

- 4 large tomatoes, diced
- 2 ripe avocados, diced
- 1/2 red onion, finely chopped
- 1/4 cup fresh cilantro, chopped
- 2 tbsp fresh lime juice
- 2 tbsp extra-virgin olive oil
- 1/2 tsp salt
- 1/4 tsp black pepper

1. In a large bowl, combine the diced tomatoes, avocados, red onion, and cilantro.
2. In a small bowl, whisk together the lime juice, olive oil, salt, and black pepper.
3. Pour the dressing over the salad and toss gently to combine.
4. Serve immediately.

Nutritional Information (per serving): Calories: 200 | Protein: 3g | Carbohydrates: 15g | Fats:17g

Fiber: 8g | Cholesterol: 0mg | Sodium: 200mg

Health Benefits: Tomato and Avocado Salad is rich in healthy fats and antioxidants, promoting heart health and reducing inflammation. The combination of fresh tomatoes and avocados provides essential vitamins and minerals, aligning with the Mediterranean Diet's emphasis on fresh, nutritious ingredients.

Spicy Chickpea Salad

Serves:4 | Prep Time:10 min | Cook Time:0 min

- 1 can (14 oz) chickpeas, drained and rinsed
- 1 red bell pepper, diced
- 1 cucumber, diced
- 1/2 red onion, finely chopped
- 1/4 cup fresh parsley, chopped
- 2 tbsp extra-virgin olive oil
- 2 tbsp fresh lemon juice
- 1 tsp ground cumin
- 1/2 tsp smoked paprika
- 1/4 tsp cayenne pepper (optional)
- 1/2 tsp salt
- 1/4 tsp black pepper

1. In a large bowl, combine the chickpeas, red bell pepper, cucumber, red onion, and parsley.
2. In a small bowl, whisk together the olive oil, lemon juice, ground cumin, smoked paprika, cayenne pepper (if using), salt, and black pepper.
3. Pour the dressing over the salad and toss to combine.
4. Serve immediately.

Nutritional Information (per serving): Calories: 180 | Protein: 6g | Carbohydrates: 22g | Fats: 8g | Fiber: 6g | Cholesterol: 0mg | Sodium: 250mg

Health Benefits: Spicy Chickpea Salad is high in fiber and plant-based protein, promoting digestive health and muscle wellness. The combination of chickpeas, fresh vegetables, and spices provides essential vitamins, minerals, and antioxidants, aligning with the Mediterranean Diet's emphasis on fresh, nutritious ingredients.

Grilled Vegetable Salad

Serves:4 | Prep Time:10 min | Cook Time:20 min

- 1 red bell pepper, sliced
- 1 yellow bell pepper, sliced
- 1 zucchini, sliced
- 1 eggplant, sliced
- 1 red onion, sliced
- 2 tbsp olive oil
- 1 tbsp balsamic vinegar
- 1 tsp dried oregano
- 1/2 tsp salt
- 1/4 tsp black pepper

- 4 cups mixed greens
- 1/4 cup crumbled feta cheese

1. Preheat your grill or grill pan over medium-high heat.
2. In a large bowl, toss the sliced vegetables with olive oil, balsamic vinegar, oregano, salt, and black pepper.
3. Grill the vegetables for 15-20 minutes, turning occasionally, until tender and slightly charred.
4. In a large salad bowl, combine the grilled vegetables and mixed greens.
5. Sprinkle with crumbled feta cheese before serving.

Nutritional Information (per serving): Calories: 220 | Protein: 5g | Carbohydrates: 18g | Fats: 15g | Fiber: 6g | Cholesterol: 10mg | Sodium: 300mg

Health Benefits: Grilled Vegetable Salad is rich in vitamins and antioxidants, promoting overall health and immune function. The combination of grilled vegetables, olive oil, and feta provides heart-healthy fats and essential nutrients, aligning with the Mediterranean Diet's principles of fresh, nutritious ingredients.

Lentil and Arugula Salad

Serves:4 | Prep Time:10 min | Cook Time:20 min

- 1 cup dried lentils, rinsed
- 2 cups water
- 4 cups arugula
- 1 pint cherry tomatoes, halved
- 1/2 red onion, thinly sliced
- 1/4 cup crumbled goat cheese
- 1/4 cup extra-virgin olive oil
- 2 tbsp red wine vinegar
- 1 tsp Dijon mustard
- 1/2 tsp salt
- 1/4 tsp black pepper

1. In a medium pot, bring the water to a boil. Add the lentils, reduce the heat to low, cover, and simmer for 20 minutes, or until tender. Drain and let cool.
2. In a large bowl, combine the cooked lentils, arugula, cherry tomatoes, and red onion.
3. In a small bowl, whisk together the olive oil, red wine vinegar, Dijon mustard, salt, and black pepper.
4. Pour the dressing over the salad and toss to combine.
5. Sprinkle with crumbled goat cheese before serving.

Nutritional Information (per serving): Calories: 250 | Protein: 10g | Carbohydrates: 20g | Fats: 15g | Fiber: 7g | Cholesterol: 10mg | Sodium: 300mg

Health Benefits: Lentil and Arugula Salad is high in fiber and plant-based protein, promoting digestive health and muscle wellness. The combination of lentils, arugula, and goat cheese provides essential vitamins, minerals, and antioxidants, aligning with the Mediterranean Diet's emphasis on fresh, nutritious ingredients.

Mediterranean Couscous Salad

Serves:4 | Prep Time:10 min | Cook Time:10 min

- 1 cup couscous
- 1 cup boiling water
- 1 cup cherry tomatoes, halved
- 1 cucumber, diced
- 1/4 cup Kalamata olives, pitted and halved
- 1/4 cup crumbled feta cheese
- 1/4 cup fresh parsley, chopped
- 2 tbsp extra-virgin olive oil
- 2 tbsp lemon juice
- 1 tsp dried oregano
- 1/2 tsp salt
- 1/4 tsp black pepper

1. In a large bowl, pour boiling water over the couscous. Cover and let sit for 5 minutes, then fluff with a fork and let cool.
2. Add the cherry tomatoes, cucumber, Kalamata olives, feta cheese, and parsley to the couscous.
3. In a small bowl, whisk together the olive oil, lemon juice, oregano, salt, and black pepper.
4. Pour the dressing over the salad and toss to combine.

Nutritional Information (per serving): Calories: 220 | Protein: 6g | Carbohydrates: 28g | Fats: 10g | Fiber: 4g | Cholesterol: 10mg | Sodium: 350mg

Health Benefits: Mediterranean Couscous Salad is rich in fiber and antioxidants, promoting digestive health and overall wellness. The combination of couscous, fresh vegetables, and olive oil provides essential vitamins and minerals, aligning with the Mediterranean Diet's principles of fresh, nutritious ingredients.

Watermelon and Feta Salad

Serves:4 | Prep Time:10 min | Cook Time:0 min

- 4 cups watermelon, cubed
- 1/2 cup crumbled feta cheese
- 1/4 cup fresh mint leaves, chopped
- 2 tbsp extra-virgin olive oil
- 2 tbsp fresh lime juice
- 1/4 tsp salt
- 1/4 tsp black pepper

1. In a large bowl, combine the watermelon cubes, feta cheese, and mint leaves.
2. In a small bowl, whisk together the olive oil, lime juice, salt, and black pepper.

3. Pour the dressing over the salad and toss gently to combine.
4. Serve immediately.

Nutritional Information (per serving): Calories: 150 | Protein: 4g | Carbohydrates: 18g | Fats: 8g | Fiber: 1g | Cholesterol: 10mg | Sodium: 200mg

Health Benefits: Watermelon and Feta Salad is hydrating and rich in antioxidants, promoting overall health and reducing inflammation. The combination of watermelon, feta, and mint provides essential vitamins and minerals, aligning with the Mediterranean Diet's emphasis on fresh, nutritious ingredients.

Citrus and Olive Salad

Serves:4 | Prep Time:10 min | Cook Time:0 min

- 2 oranges, peeled and sliced
- 2 grapefruits, peeled and sliced
- 1/4 cup Kalamata olives, pitted and halved
- 1/4 red onion, thinly sliced
- 1/4 cup fresh mint leaves, chopped
- 2 tbsp extra-virgin olive oil
- 1 tbsp red wine vinegar
- 1 tsp honey
- 1/4 tsp salt
- 1/4 tsp black peppe

1. In a large bowl, combine the orange slices, grapefruit slices, Kalamata olives, red onion, and mint leaves.
2. In a small bowl, whisk together the olive oil, red wine vinegar, honey, salt, and black pepper.
3. Pour the dressing over the salad and toss gently to combine.
4. Serve immediately.

Nutritional Information (per serving): Calories: 170 | Protein: 2g | Carbohydrates: 24g | Fats: 8g | Fiber: 4g | Cholesterol: 0mg | Sodium: 150mg

Health Benefits: Citrus and Olive Salad is rich in vitamins and antioxidants, promoting immune function and overall health. The combination of citrus fruits, olives, and mint provides essential nutrients and heart-healthy fats, aligning with the Mediterranean Diet's emphasis on fresh, nutritious ingredients.

Kale and Chickpea Salad

Serves:4 | Prep Time:10 min | Cook Time:0 min

- 4 cups kale, chopped
- 1 can (14 oz) chickpeas, drained and rinsed
- 1/2 red bell pepper, diced
- 1/4 cup sunflower seeds
- 1/4 cup crumbled feta cheese
- 1/4 cup extra-virgin olive oil
- 2 tbsp lemon juice
- 1 tbsp Dijon mustard
- 1/2 tsp salt
- 1/4 tsp black pepper

1. In a large bowl, combine the chopped kale, chickpeas, red bell pepper, sunflower seeds, and feta cheese.
2. In a small bowl, whisk together the olive oil, lemon juice, Dijon mustard, salt, and black pepper.
3. Pour the dressing over the salad and toss to combine.
4. Serve immediately.

Nutritional Information (per serving): Calories: 250 | Protein: 8g | Carbohydrates: 20g | Fats: 16g | Fiber: 6g | Cholesterol: 10mg | Sodium: 300mg

Health Benefits: Kale and Chickpea Salad is high in fiber and plant-based protein, promoting digestive health and muscle wellness. The combination of kale, chickpeas, and sunflower seeds provides essential vitamins, minerals, and antioxidants, aligning with the Mediterranean Diet's emphasis on fresh, nutritious ingredients.

CHAPTER 10

DESSERTS - INDULGENT YET HEALTHY SWEETS

Greek Yogurt with Honey and Walnuts

Serves:4 | Prep Time:5 min | Cook Time:0 min

- 2 cups Greek yogurt
- 1/4 cup honey
- 1/2 cup walnuts, chopped
- 1 tsp ground cinnamon (optional)

1. Divide the Greek yogurt evenly among four bowls.
2. Drizzle each serving with honey.
3. Sprinkle with chopped walnuts.
4. Optional: Dust with ground cinnamon before serving.

Nutritional Information (per serving): Calories: 200 | Protein: 10g | Carbohydrates: 20g | Fats: 10g | Fiber: 2g | Cholesterol: 5mg | Sodium: 50mg

Health Benefits: Greek Yogurt with Honey and Walnuts is rich in protein and healthy fats, promoting muscle health and providing sustained energy. The combination of Greek yogurt, honey, and walnuts provides essential vitamins minerals, and antioxidants, aligning with the Mediterranean Diet's emphasis on fresh, nutritious ingredients.

Lemon Olive Oil Cake

Serves:8 | Prep Time:15 min | Cook Time:30 min

- 1 1/2 cups all-purpose flour
- 1 cup sugar
- 1/2 tsp baking powder
- 1/2 tsp baking soda
- 1/4 tsp salt
- 3/4 cup extra-virgin olive oil
- 3 large eggs
- 1/2 cup plain Greek yogurt
- 1/4 cup fresh lemon juice
- 1 tbsp lemon zest
- 1 tsp vanilla extract
- Powdered sugar (for dusting, optional)

1. Preheat your oven to 350°F (175°C). Grease and flour a 9-inch round cake pan.
2. In a large bowl, whisk together the flour, sugar, baking powder, baking soda, and salt.
3. In another bowl, whisk together the olive oil, eggs, Greek yogurt, lemon juice, lemon zest, and vanilla extract.

4. Add the wet ingredients to the dry ingredients and mix until just combined.
5. Pour the batter into the prepared cake pan and smooth the top.
6. Bake in the preheated oven for 30 minutes, or until a toothpick inserted into the center comes out clean.
7. Let the cake cool in the pan for 10 minutes, then transfer to a wire rack to cool completely.
8. Optional: Dust with powdered sugar before serving.

Nutritional Information (per serving): Calories: 300 | Protein: 5g | Carbohydrates: 30g | Fats: 18g | Fiber: 1g | Cholesterol: 60mg | Sodium: 150mg

Health Benefits: Lemon Olive Oil Cake is a lighter dessert option rich in healthy fats and antioxidants, promoting heart health. The combination of olive oil, lemon, and Greek yogurt provides essential vitamins and minerals, aligning with the Mediterranean Diet's emphasis on fresh, nutritious ingredients.

Pistachio Baklava Bites

Serves:12 | Prep Time:15 min | Cook Time:15 min

- 1 cup shelled pistachios, finely chopped
- 1/4 cup sugar
- 1 tsp ground cinnamon
- 12 sheets phyllo dough, thawed
- 1/2 cup unsalted butter, melted
- 1/2 cup honey
- 1 tsp lemon juice

1. Preheat your oven to 350°F (175°C). Line a muffin tin with paper liners.
2. In a bowl, combine the chopped pistachios, sugar, and ground cinnamon.
3. Place one sheet of phyllo dough on a clean surface and brush with melted butter. Repeat with two more sheets, stacking them. Cut the stack into four equal squares.
4. Press each phyllo square into a muffin cup, creating a small cup shape. Repeat with the remaining phyllo sheets.
5. Fill each phyllo cup with the pistachio mixture.
6. Bake in the preheated oven for 15 minutes, or until golden brown.

7. In a small saucepan, heat the honey and lemon juice over low heat until warm. Drizzle over the baklava bites before serving.

Nutritional Information (per serving): Calories: 200 | Protein: 3g | Carbohydrates: 25g | Fats: 10g | Fiber: 1g | Cholesterol: 15mg | Sodium: 50mg

Health Benefits: Pistachio Baklava Bites are a delicious treat rich in healthy fats and antioxidants, promoting heart health and providing sustained energy. The combination of pistachios, honey, and phyllo dough provides essential vitamins and minerals, aligning with the Mediterranean Diet's emphasis on fresh, nutritious ingredients.

Fig and Almond Tart

Serves:8 | Prep Time:20 min | Cook Time:25 min

- 1 sheet puff pastry, thawed
- 8 fresh figs, sliced
- 1/2 cup almond flour
- 1/4 cup sugar
- 1/4 cup unsalted butter, softened
- 1 large egg
- 1 tsp vanilla extract
- 1/4 cup sliced almonds
- Honey (for drizzling, optional)

1. Preheat your oven to 375°F (190°C). Line a baking sheet with parchment paper.
2. Roll out the puff pastry sheet on a lightly floured surface and transfer to the prepared baking sheet.
3. In a bowl, cream together the almond flour, sugar, butter, egg, and vanilla extract until smooth.
4. Spread the almond mixture evenly over the puff pastry, leaving a 1-inch border around the edges.
5. Arrange the fig slices on top of the almond mixture.
6. Fold the edges of the puff pastry over the filling to create a border.
7. Sprinkle the sliced almonds over the top.
8. Bake in the preheated oven for 25 minutes, or until the pastry is golden brown.
9. Optional: Drizzle with honey before serving.

Nutritional Information (per serving): Calories: 300 | Protein: 5g | Carbohydrates: 35g | Fats: 18g | Fiber: 3g | Cholesterol: 30mg | Sodium: 75mg

Health Benefits: Fig and Almond Tart is rich in fiber and healthy fats, promoting digestive health and heart health. The combination of figs, almonds, and puff pastry provides essential vitamins and minerals, aligning with the Mediterranean Diet's emphasis on fresh, nutritious ingredients.

Honey Poached Pears

Serves:4 | Prep Time:10 min | Cook Time:20 min

- 4 ripe pears, peeled and cored
- 4 cups water
- 1/2 cup honey
- 1 cinnamon stick
- 1 vanilla bean, split and seeds scraped
- 2 tbsp lemon juice
- Fresh mint leaves (for garnish)

1. In a large saucepan, combine the water, honey, cinnamon stick, vanilla bean, and lemon juice. Bring to a simmer over medium heat.
2. Add the pears to the saucepan and simmer for 15-20 minutes, or until the pears are tender.
3. Remove the pears from the poaching liquid and let cool slightly.
4. Serve the pears warm or chilled, garnished with fresh mint leaves.

Nutritional Information (per serving): Calories: 150 | Protein: 1g | Carbohydrates: 38g | Fats: 0g | Fiber: 4g | Cholesterol: 0mg | Sodium: 5mg

Health Benefits: Honey Poached Pears are a light and healthy dessert rich in natural sugars and antioxidants, promoting digestive health and reducing inflammation. The combination of pears, honey, and spices provides essential vitamins and minerals, aligning with the Mediterranean Diet's emphasis on fresh, nutritious ingredients.

Orange and Olive Oil Muffins

Serves:12 | Prep Time:15 min | Cook Time:20 min

- 1 1/2 cups all-purpose flour
- 1/2 cup sugar
- 1 tsp baking powder
- 1/2 tsp baking soda
- 1/4 tsp salt
- 1/2 cup extra-virgin olive oil
- 2 large eggs
- 1/2 cup fresh orange juice
- 1 tbsp orange zest
- 1 tsp vanilla extract

1. Preheat your oven to 350°F (175°C). Line a muffin tin with paper liners.
2. In a large bowl, whisk together the flour, sugar, baking powder, baking soda, and salt.
3. In another bowl, whisk together the olive oil, eggs, orange juice, orange zest, and vanilla extract.
4. Add the wet ingredients to the dry ingredients and mix until just combined.
5. Divide the batter evenly among the muffin cups.
6. Bake in the preheated oven for 20 minutes, or until a toothpick inserted into the center comes out clean.

- Let the muffins cool in the tin for 5 minutes, then transfer to a wire rack to cool completely.

Nutritional Information (per serving): Calories: 180 | Protein: 3g | Carbohydrates: 22g | Fats: 9g | Fiber: 1g | Cholesterol: 30mg | Sodium: 150mg

Health Benefits: Orange and Olive Oil Muffins are a delicious treat rich in healthy fats and antioxidants, promoting heart health. The combination of olive oil, orange juice, and zest provides essential vitamins and minerals, aligning with the Mediterranean Diet's emphasis on fresh, nutritious ingredients.

Greek Yogurt Cheesecake

Serves:8 | Prep Time:15 min | Cook Time:30 min

- 1 1/2 cups graham cracker crumbs
- 1/4 cup unsalted butter, melted
- 2 cups Greek yogurt
- 1/2 cup sugar
- 2 large eggs
- 1 tsp vanilla extract
- 1 tbsp lemon juice
- Fresh berries (for topping)

1. Preheat your oven to 350°F (175°C). Grease a 9-inch springform pan.
2. In a bowl, mix the graham cracker crumbs with the melted butter until well combined. Press the mixture into the bottom of the prepared pan to form the crust.
3. In a large bowl, beat the Greek yogurt, sugar, eggs, vanilla extract, and lemon juice until smooth.
4. Pour the yogurt mixture over the crust and smooth the top.
5. Bake in the preheated oven for 30 minutes, or until the cheesecake is set.
6. Let the cheesecake cool in the pan, then refrigerate for at least 2 hours before serving.
7. Top with fresh berries before serving.

Nutritional Information (per serving): Calories: 220 | Protein: 8g | Carbohydrates: 28g | Fats: 10g | Fiber: 1g | Cholesterol: 60mg | Sodium: 150mg

Health Benefits: Greek Yogurt Cheesecake is a lighter alternative to traditional cheesecake, rich in protein and healthy fats. The combination of Greek yogurt and fresh berries provides essential vitamins, minerals, and antioxidants, aligning with the Mediterranean Diet's emphasis on fresh, nutritious ingredients.

Lemon Poppy Seed Muffins

Serves:12 | Prep Time:15 min | Cook Time:20 min

- 1 1/2 cups all-purpose flour
- 1/2 cup sugar
- 1 tbsp poppy seeds
- 1 tsp baking powder
- 1/2 tsp baking soda
- 1/4 tsp salt
- 1/2 cup unsalted butter, melted
- 2 large eggs
- 1/2 cup plain Greek yogurt
- 1/4 cup fresh lemon juice
- 1 tbsp lemon zest
- 1 tsp vanilla extract

1. Preheat your oven to 350°F (175°C). Line a muffin tin with paper liners.
2. In a large bowl, whisk together the flour, sugar, poppy seeds, baking powder, baking soda, and salt.
3. In another bowl, whisk together the melted butter, eggs, Greek yogurt, lemon juice, lemon zest, and vanilla extract.
4. Add the wet ingredients to the dry ingredients and mix until just combined.
5. Divide the batter evenly among the muffin cups.
6. Bake in the preheated oven for 20 minutes, or until a toothpick inserted into the center comes out clean.
7. Let the muffins cool in the tin for 5 minutes, then transfer to a wire rack to cool completely.

Nutritional Information (per serving): Calories: 200 | Protein: 4g | Carbohydrates: 22g | Fats: 10g | Fiber: 1g | Cholesterol: 50mg | Sodium: 150mg

Health Benefits: Lemon Poppy Seed Muffins are a refreshing treat rich in antioxidants and healthy fats, promoting overall wellness. The combination of lemon juice, zest, and poppy seeds provides essential vitamins and minerals, aligning with the Mediterranean Diet's emphasis on fresh, nutritious ingredients.

Almond and Orange Biscotti

Serves:12 | Prep Time:15 min | Cook Time:30 min

- 1 3/4 cups all-purpose flour
- 1 cup sugar
- 1 tsp baking powder
- 1/4 tsp salt
- 3 large eggs
- 1 tsp vanilla extract
- 1 tbsp orange zest
- 1 cup whole almonds, toasted
- 1/2 cup sliced almonds

1. Preheat your oven to 350°F (175°C). Line a baking sheet with parchment paper.

2. In a large bowl, whisk together the flour, sugar, baking powder, and salt.

3. In another bowl, beat the eggs, vanilla extract, and orange zest until combined.

4. Add the wet ingredients to the dry ingredients and mix until just combined. Fold in the whole almonds.

5. Divide the dough in half and shape each half into a log about 12 inches long and 2 inches wide. Place the logs on the prepared baking sheet and flatten slightly.

6. Bake in the preheated oven for 25 minutes, or until golden brown. Let cool for 10 minutes.

7. Using a serrated knife, cut the logs into 1/2-inch-thick slices. Place the slices cut-side down on the baking sheet and bake for an additional 10 minutes, or until crisp.

8. Let cool completely and store in an airtight container.

Nutritional Information (per serving): Calories: 180 | Protein: 4g | Carbohydrates: 25g | Fats: 7g | Fiber: 2g | Cholesterol: 35mg | Sodium: 80mg

Health Benefits: Almond and Orange Biscotti are a delicious treat rich in healthy fats and antioxidants, promoting heart health and providing sustained energy. The combination of almonds, orange zest, and whole grains provides essential vitamins and minerals, aligning with the Mediterranean Diet's emphasis on fresh, nutritious ingredients.

Spiced Honey Almonds

Serves:4 | Prep Time:5 min | Cook Time:10 min

- 2 cups whole almonds
- 2 tbsp honey
- 1 tbsp olive oil
- 1 tsp ground cinnamon
- 1/2 tsp ground cumin
- 1/4 tsp cayenne pepper (optional)
- 1/4 tsp salt

1. Preheat your oven to 350°F (175°C). Line a baking sheet with parchment paper.

2. In a large bowl, combine the honey, olive oil, cinnamon, cumin, cayenne pepper (if using), and salt.

3. Add the almonds to the bowl and toss to coat.

4. Spread the almonds in a single layer on the prepared baking sheet.

5. Bake in the preheated oven for 10 minutes, stirring halfway through, until the almonds are golden brown and fragrant.

6. Let cool completely before serving.

Nutritional Information (per serving): Calories: 250 | Protein: 6g | Carbohydrates: 15g | Fats: 18g | Fiber: 4g | Cholesterol: 0mg | Sodium: 100mg

Health Benefits: Spiced Honey Almonds are a nutritious snack rich in healthy fats and antioxidants, promoting heart health and providing sustained energy. The combination of almonds, honey, and spices provides essential vitamins and minerals, aligning with the Mediterranean Diet's emphasis on fresh, nutritious ingredients.

Greek Semolina Cake

Serves:8 | Prep Time:15 min | Cook Time:30 min

- 1 cup semolina flour
- 1/2 cup all-purpose flour
- 1 cup sugar
- 1/2 cup unsalted butter, melted
- 1 cup Greek yogurt
- 2 large eggs
- 1 tsp baking powder
- 1/2 tsp baking soda
- 1/4 tsp salt
- 1 tsp vanilla extract
- 1/4 cup honey
- 1/4 cup water
- 1 tbsp lemon juice

1. Preheat your oven to 350°F (175°C). Grease and flour a 9-inch round cake pan.

2. In a large bowl, whisk together the semolina flour, all-purpose flour, sugar, baking powder, baking soda, and salt.

3. In another bowl, beat the melted butter, Greek yogurt, eggs, and vanilla extract until smooth.

4. Add the wet ingredients to the dry ingredients and mix until just combined.

5. Pour the batter into the prepared cake pan and smooth the top.

6. Bake in the preheated oven for 30 minutes, or until a toothpick inserted into the center comes out clean.

7. In a small saucepan, combine the honey, water, and lemon juice. Bring to a simmer over low heat, stirring until the honey is dissolved.

8. Pour the warm honey syrup over the cake as soon as it comes out of the oven. Let the cake cool in the pan before serving.

Nutritional Information (per serving): Calories: 280 | Protein: 5g | Carbohydrates: 38g | Fats: 12g | Fiber: 1g | Cholesterol: 60mg | Sodium: 150mg

Health Benefits: Greek Semolina Cake is a delicious dessert rich in healthy fats and antioxidants, promoting heart health and providing sustained energy. The combination of semolina, Greek yogurt, and honey provides essential vitamins and minerals, aligning with the Mediterranean Diet's emphasis on fresh, nutritious ingredients.

Lemon and Rosemary Shortbread

Serves:12 | Prep Time:15 min | Cook Time:20 min

- 1 cup unsalted butter, softened
- 1/2 cup powdered sugar
- 2 cups all-purpose flour
- 1 tbsp lemon zest
- 1 tbsp fresh rosemary, finely chopped
- 1/4 tsp salt

1. Preheat your oven to 350°F (175°C). Line a baking sheet with parchment paper.
2. In a large bowl, cream together the softened butter and powdered sugar until light and fluffy.
3. Add the flour, lemon zest, rosemary, and salt. Mix until just combined.
4. Roll the dough into a log and wrap in plastic wrap. Refrigerate for 30 minutes.
5. Slice the dough into 1/4-inch-thick rounds and place them on the prepared baking sheet.
6. Bake in the preheated oven for 15-20 minutes, or until the edges are golden brown.
7. Let cool completely before serving.

Nutritional Information (per serving): Calories: 150 | Protein: 2g | Carbohydrates: 16g | Fats: 9g | Fiber: 1g | Cholesterol: 25mg | Sodium: 50mg

Health Benefits: Lemon and Rosemary Shortbread is a delightful treat rich in antioxidants and healthy fats, promoting heart health. The combination of lemon zest and rosemary provides essential vitamins and minerals, aligning with the Mediterranean Diet's emphasis on fresh, nutritious ingredients.

Apricot and Almond Clafoutis

Serves:8 | Prep Time:15 min | Cook Time:35 min

- 1 cup whole milk
- 1/2 cup heavy cream
- 3 large eggs
- 1/2 cup sugar
- 1 tsp vanilla extract
- 1/4 tsp almond extract
- 1/2 cup all-purpose flour
- 1/4 tsp salt
- 1 lb fresh apricots, halved and pitted
- 1/4 cup sliced almonds
- Powdered sugar (for dusting, optional)

1. Preheat your oven to 350°F (175°C). Grease a 9-inch pie dish or baking dish.
2. In a large bowl, whisk together the milk, heavy cream, eggs, sugar, vanilla extract, and almond extract until smooth.
3. Gradually add the flour and salt, whisking until just combined.
4. Arrange the apricot halves in the prepared baking dish, cut-side up.
5. Pour the batter over the apricots and sprinkle with sliced almonds.
6. Bake in the preheated oven for 35 minutes, or until the clafoutis is set and golden brown.
7. Let cool slightly, then dust with powdered sugar before serving.

Nutritional Information (per serving): Calories: 200 | Protein: 5g | Carbohydrates: 25g | Fats: 10g | Fiber: 2g | Cholesterol: 80mg | Sodium: 60mg

Health Benefits: Apricot and Almond Clafoutis is a delightful dessert rich in fiber and antioxidants, promoting digestive health and providing essential vitamins and minerals. The combination of fresh apricots, almonds, and dairy aligns with the Mediterranean Diet's emphasis on fresh, nutritious ingredients.

Olive Oil and Citrus Cookies

Serves:12 | Prep Time:15 min | Cook Time:15 min

- 1/2 cup extra-virgin olive oil
- 1/2 cup sugar
- 1 large egg
- 1 tsp vanilla extract
- 1 tbsp orange zest
- 1 tbsp lemon zest
- 1 1/2 cups all-purpose flour
- 1/2 tsp baking powder
- 1/4 tsp salt

1. Preheat your oven to 350°F (175°C). Line a baking sheet with parchment paper.
2. In a large bowl, whisk together the olive oil and sugar until well combined.
3. Add the egg, vanilla extract, orange zest, and lemon zest, and whisk until smooth.
4. In another bowl, whisk together the flour, baking powder, and salt.
5. Gradually add the dry ingredients to the wet ingredients, mixing until just combined.
6. Drop spoonfuls of dough onto the prepared baking sheet, spacing them about 2 inches apart.
7. Bake in the preheated oven for 12-15 minutes, or until the edges are golden brown.
8. Let the cookies cool on the baking sheet for 5 minutes, then transfer to a wire rack to cool completely.

Nutritional Information (per serving): Calories: 150 | Protein: 2g | Carbohydrates: 20g | Fats: 7g | Fiber: 1g | Cholesterol: 15mg | Sodium: 50mg

Health Benefits: Olive Oil and Citrus Cookies are a refreshing treat rich in antioxidants and healthy fats, promoting heart health and overall wellness. The combination of olive oil, citrus zest, and whole grains provides essential vitamins and minerals, aligning with the Mediterranean Diet's emphasis on fresh, nutritious ingredients.

Chocolate-Dipped Figs

Serves:12 | Prep Time:10 min | Cook Time:10 min

- 12 fresh figs, washed and dried
- 1 cup dark chocolate chips
- 1 tbsp coconut oil
- 1/4 cup chopped pistachios (optional)

1. Line a baking sheet with parchment paper.
2. In a microwave-safe bowl, combine the dark chocolate chips and coconut oil. Microwave in 30-second intervals, stirring after each, until the chocolate is melted and smooth.
3. Dip each fig halfway into the melted chocolate, allowing the excess to drip off.
4. Place the chocolate-dipped figs on the prepared baking sheet.
5. Optional: Sprinkle the chocolate with chopped pistachios before the chocolate sets.
6. Refrigerate the figs for 10-15 minutes, or until the chocolate is firm.
7. Serve chilled or at room temperature.

Nutritional Information (per serving): Calories: 100 | Protein: 1g | Carbohydrates: 15g | Fats: 5g | Fiber: 2g | Cholesterol: 0mg | Sodium: 5mg

Health Benefits: Chocolate-Dipped Figs are a delightful and healthy treat rich in antioxidants and fiber, promoting heart health and digestive wellness. The combination of figs, dark chocolate, and pistachios provides essential vitamins and minerals, aligning with the Mediterranean Diet's emphasis on fresh, nutritious ingredients.

CHAPTER 11

PASTA - CLASSIC AND CREATIVE PASTA DISHES

Lemon Garlic Shrimp Pasta

Serves:4 | Prep Time:10 min | Cook Time:15 min

- 8 oz spaghetti
- 2 tbsp olive oil
- 4 cloves garlic, minced
- 1 lb shrimp, peeled and deveined
- 1/4 cup fresh lemon juice
- 1/4 cup grated Parmesan cheese
- 1/4 cup fresh parsley, chopped
- 1/2 tsp salt
- 1/4 tsp black pepper
- Lemon zest (for garnish)

1. Cook the spaghetti according to package instructions. Drain and set aside.
2. In a large skillet, heat the olive oil over medium heat. Add the garlic and sauté until fragrant, about 1 minute.
3. Add the shrimp to the skillet and cook until pink and opaque, about 3-4 minutes.
4. Stir in the lemon juice, Parmesan cheese, parsley, salt, and black pepper.
5. Add the cooked spaghetti to the skillet and toss to combine.
6. Garnish with lemon zest before serving.

Nutritional Information (per serving): Calories: 400 | Protein: 30g | Carbohydrates: 45g | Fats: 12g | Fiber: 3g | Cholesterol: 200mg | Sodium: 600mg

Health Benefits: Lemon Garlic Shrimp Pasta is a light and flavorful dish rich in protein and healthy fats, promoting muscle health and heart health. The combination of shrimp, garlic, and lemon provides essential vitamins and minerals, aligning with the Mediterranean Diet's emphasis on fresh, nutritious ingredients.

Mediterranean Penne with Artichokes

Serves:4 | Prep Time:10 min | Cook Time:15 min

- 8 oz penne pasta
- 2 tbsp olive oil
- 1 small onion, chopped
- 2 cloves garlic, minced
- 1 can (14 oz) artichoke hearts, drained and quartered
- 1 cup cherry tomatoes, halved
- 1/2 cup Kalamata olives, pitted and halved
- 1/4 cup crumbled feta cheese
- 1/4 cup fresh basil, chopped
- 1/2 tsp dried oregano
- 1/2 tsp salt
- 1/4 tsp black pepper

1. Cook the penne pasta according to package instructions. Drain and set aside.
2. In a large skillet, heat the olive oil over medium heat. Add the onion and garlic, and sauté until softened, about 3 minutes.
3. Add the artichoke hearts, cherry tomatoes, and Kalamata olives to the skillet. Cook for 5 minutes, stirring occasionally.
4. Stir in the cooked penne, feta cheese, basil, oregano, salt, and black pepper. Toss to combine.
5. Serve hot.

Nutritional Information (per serving): Calories: 380 | Protein: 10g | Carbohydrates: 55g | Fats: 15g | Fiber: 6g | Cholesterol: 15mg | Sodium: 500mg

Health Benefits: Mediterranean Penne with Artichokes is a delicious and nutritious dish rich in fiber and antioxidants, promoting overall health and immune function. The combination of artichokes, tomatoes, and olives provides essential vitamins and minerals, aligning with the Mediterranean Diet's emphasis on fresh, nutritious ingredients.

Greek-Style Spaghetti

Serves:4 | Prep Time:10 min | Cook Time:15 min

- 8 oz spaghetti
- 2 tbsp olive oil
- 1 small onion, chopped
- 2 cloves garlic, minced
- 1 can (14 oz) diced tomatoes
- 1/2 cup Kalamata olives, pitted and halved
- 1/4 cup crumbled feta cheese
- 1/4 cup fresh parsley, chopped
- 1 tsp dried oregano
- 1/2 tsp salt
- 1/4 tsp black pepper

1. Cook the spaghetti according to package instructions. Drain and set aside.
2. In a large skillet, heat the olive oil over medium heat. Add the onion and garlic, and sauté until softened, about 3 minutes.

- 3. Add the diced tomatoes, Kalamata olives, oregano, salt, and black pepper to the skillet. Cook for 10 minutes, stirring occasionally.
- 4. Stir in the cooked spaghetti and toss to combine.
- 5. Top with crumbled feta cheese and fresh parsley before serving.

Nutritional Information (per serving): Calories: 360 | Protein: 10g | Carbohydrates: 55g | Fats: 12g | Fiber: 5g | Cholesterol: 10mg | Sodium: 550mg

Health Benefits: Greek-Style Spaghetti is a flavorful and healthy dish rich in fiber and antioxidants, promoting overall health and digestive wellness. The combination of tomatoes, olives, and feta provides essential vitamins and minerals, aligning with the Mediterranean Diet's emphasis on fresh, nutritious ingredients.

Roasted Red Pepper Alfredo

Serves:4 | Prep Time:10 min | Cook Time:15 min

- 8 oz fettuccine
- 2 tbsp olive oil
- 4 cloves garlic, minced
- 1 jar (12 oz) roasted red peppers, drained and pureed
- 1 cup heavy cream
- 1/2 cup grated Parmesan cheese
- 1/4 tsp red pepper flakes (optional)
- 1/2 tsp salt
- 1/4 tsp black pepper
- Fresh basil, chopped (for garnish)

1. Cook the fettuccine according to package instructions. Drain and set aside.
2. In a large skillet, heat the olive oil over medium heat. Add the garlic and sauté until fragrant, about 1 minute.
3. Stir in the pureed roasted red peppers, heavy cream, Parmesan cheese, red pepper flakes (if using), salt, and black pepper. Cook for 5 minutes, stirring occasionally, until the sauce thickens.
4. Add the cooked fettuccine to the skillet and toss to coat with the sauce.
5. Garnish with fresh basil before serving.

Nutritional Information (per serving): Calories: 450 | Protein: 12g | Carbohydrates: 50g | Fats: 22g | Fiber: 3g | Cholesterol: 70mg | Sodium: 600mg

Health Benefits: Roasted Red Pepper Alfredo is a creamy and flavorful dish rich in healthy fats and antioxidants, promoting heart health and overall wellness. The combination of roasted red peppers and garlic provides essential vitamins and minerals, aligning with the Mediterranean Diet's emphasis on fresh, nutritious ingredients.

Spinach and Feta Stuffed Shells

Serves:4 | Prep Time:15 min | Cook Time:25 min

- 20 jumbo pasta shells
- 1 tbsp olive oil
- 1 small onion, chopped
- 2 cloves garlic, minced
- 10 oz frozen spinach, thawed and drained
- 1 cup ricotta cheese
- 1 cup crumbled feta cheese
- 1 egg, beaten
- 1 tsp dried oregano
- 1/2 tsp salt
- 1/4 tsp black pepper
- 2 cups marinara sauce
- 1/4 cup grated Parmesan cheese

1. Preheat your oven to 375°F (190°C). Grease a baking dish with olive oil.
2. Cook the pasta shells according to package instructions. Drain and set aside.
3. In a large skillet, heat the olive oil over medium heat. Add the onion and garlic, and sauté until softened, about 3 minutes.
4. Add the spinach to the skillet and cook for another 2 minutes. Remove from heat and let cool slightly.
5. In a large bowl, combine the ricotta cheese, feta cheese, egg, oregano, salt, and black pepper. Stir in the spinach mixture.
6. Stuff each pasta shell with the spinach and cheese mixture and place them in the prepared baking dish.
7. Pour the marinara sauce over the stuffed shells and sprinkle with grated Parmesan cheese.
8. Bake in the preheated oven for 25 minutes, or until the sauce is bubbling and the cheese is melted.
9. Serve hot.

Nutritional Information (per serving): Calories: 350 | Protein: 18g | Carbohydrates: 35g | Fats: 18g | Fiber: 5g | Cholesterol: 80mg | Sodium: 800mg

Health Benefits: Spinach and Feta Stuffed Shells are rich in protein and fiber, promoting muscle health and digestive wellness. The combination of spinach, feta, and ricotta provides essential vitamins and minerals, aligning with the Mediterranean Diet's emphasis on fresh, nutritious ingredients.

Lemon Basil Pesto Pasta

Serves:4 | Prep Time:10 min | Cook Time:10 min

- 8 oz spaghetti
- 2 cups fresh basil leaves
- 1/4 cup pine nuts
- 1/2 cup grated Parmesan cheese
- 2 cloves garlic
- 1/2 cup extra-virgin olive oil
- 1/4 cup fresh lemon juice
- 1 tsp lemon zest
- 1/2 tsp salt
- 1/4 tsp black pepper
- 1. Cook the spaghetti according to package instructions. Drain and set aside.
- 2. In a food processor, combine the basil leaves, pine nuts, Parmesan cheese, and garlic. Pulse until finely chopped.
- 3. With the food processor running, slowly add the olive oil and lemon juice until the mixture is smooth and creamy.
- 4. Stir in the lemon zest, salt, and black pepper.
- 5. Toss the cooked spaghetti with the pesto sauce until evenly coated.
- 6. Serve immediately, garnished with additional Parmesan cheese if desired.
-
- Nutritional Information (per serving): Calories: 400 | Protein: 10g | Carbohydrates: 45g | Fats: 22g | Fiber: 3g | Cholesterol: 10mg | Sodium: 350mg
-
- Health Benefits: It is a fresh and flavorful dish rich in healthy fats and antioxidants, promoting heart health and overall wellness. The combination of basil, pine nuts, and lemon provides essential vitamins and minerals.

Mediterranean Orzo with Vegetables

Serves:4 | Prep Time:10 min | Cook Time:15 min

- 1 cup orzo pasta
- 2 tbsp olive oil
- 1 small onion, chopped
- 2 cloves garlic, minced
- 1 red bell pepper, chopped
- 1 zucchini, diced
- 1/2 cup cherry tomatoes, halved
- 1/4 cup Kalamata olives, pitted and halved
- 1/4 cup crumbled feta cheese
- 1/4 cup fresh parsley, chopped
- 1 tsp dried oregano
- 1/2 tsp salt
- 1/4 tsp black pepper

1. Cook the orzo pasta according to package instructions. Drain and set aside.
2. In a large skillet, heat the olive oil over medium heat. Add the onion and garlic, and sauté until softened, about 3 minutes.
3. Add the red bell pepper and zucchini to the skillet. Cook for 5 minutes, stirring occasionally.
4. Stir in the cherry tomatoes and Kalamata olives. Cook for another 2 minutes.
5. Add the cooked orzo, feta cheese, parsley, oregano, salt, and black pepper to the skillet. Toss to combine.
6. Serve hot.

Nutritional Information (per serving): Calories: 300 | Protein: 8g | Carbohydrates: 40g | Fats: 12g | Fiber: 4g | Cholesterol: 10mg | Sodium: 400mg

Health Benefits: Mediterranean Orzo with Vegetables is rich in fiber and antioxidants, which support digestive health and boost immune function. It also supports heart health due to its healthy fats and can contribute to better energy levels with its nutrient-dense ingredients.

Spicy Tomato and Olive Pasta

Serves:4 | Prep Time:10 min | Cook Time:15 min

- 8 oz penne pasta
- 2 tbsp olive oil
- 4 cloves garlic, minced
- 1 can (14 oz) diced tomatoes
- 1/2 cup Kalamata olives, pitted and halved
- 1/4 cup tomato paste
- 1/2 tsp red pepper flakes
- 1 tsp dried oregano
- 1/2 tsp salt
- 1/4 tsp black pepper
- Fresh basil, chopped (for garnish)

1. Cook the penne pasta according to package instructions. Drain and set aside.
2. In a large skillet, heat the olive oil over medium heat. Add the garlic and sauté until fragrant, about 1 minute.
3. Stir in the diced tomatoes, Kalamata olives, tomato paste, red pepper flakes, oregano, salt, and black pepper. Cook for 10 minutes, stirring occasionally.
4. Add the cooked penne to the skillet and toss to coat with the sauce.
5. Garnish with fresh basil before serving.

Nutritional Information (per serving): Calories: 350 | Protein: 10g | Carbohydrates: 55g | Fats: 12g | Fiber: 5g | Cholesterol: 0mg | Sodium: 550mg

Health Benefits: Spicy Tomato and Olive Pasta is a flavorful dish rich in antioxidants and healthy fats, promoting heart health and overall wellness. The combination of tomatoes, olives, and spices provides essential vitamins and minerals, aligning with the Mediterranean Diet's emphasis on fresh, nutritious ingredients.

Baked Ziti with Feta

Serves:4 | Prep Time:10 min | Cook Time:20 min

- 8 oz ziti pasta
- 2 tbsp olive oil
- 2 cloves garlic, minced
- 1 can (14 oz) diced tomatoes
- 1/2 cup Kalamata olives, pitted and halved
- 1 tsp dried oregano
- 1/2 tsp salt
- 1/4 tsp black pepper
- 1 cup crumbled feta cheese
- 1/4 cup grated Parmesan cheese
- Fresh basil, chopped (for garnish)

1. Preheat your oven to 375°F (190°C). Grease a baking dish with olive oil.
2. Cook the ziti pasta according to package instructions. Drain and set aside.
3. In a large skillet, heat the olive oil over medium heat. Add the garlic and sauté until fragrant, about 1 minute.
4. Stir in the diced tomatoes, Kalamata olives, oregano, salt, and black pepper. Cook for 5 minutes, stirring occasionally.
5. Add the cooked ziti to the skillet and toss to combine.
6. Transfer the pasta mixture to the prepared baking dish. Sprinkle with crumbled feta and grated Parmesan cheese.
7. Bake in the preheated oven for 15 minutes, or until the cheese is melted and bubbly.
8. Garnish with fresh basil before serving.

Nutritional Information (per serving): Calories: 400 | Protein: 12g | Carbohydrates: 50g | Fats: 18g | Fiber: 5g | Cholesterol: 25mg | Sodium: 600mg

Health Benefits: Baked Ziti with Feta is a flavorful and nutritious dish rich in fiber and antioxidants, promoting heart health and overall wellness. The combination of ziti, tomatoes, and feta provides essential vitamins and minerals, aligning with the Mediterranean Diet's emphasis on fresh, nutritious ingredients.

Roasted Garlic and Spinach Pasta

Serves:4 | Prep Time:10 min | Cook Time:20 min

- 8 oz spaghetti
- 1/4 cup olive oil
- 1 head of garlic, cloves separated and peeled
- 1/2 tsp red pepper flakes
- 10 oz fresh spinach
- 1/4 cup grated Parmesan cheese
- 1/4 tsp salt
- 1/4 tsp black pepper

1. Preheat your oven to 375°F (190°C).

2. Place the garlic cloves on a baking sheet and drizzle with 1 tablespoon of olive oil. Roast in the preheated oven for 15 minutes, or until golden brown and tender.
3. Cook the spaghetti according to package instructions. Drain and set aside.
4. In a large skillet, heat the remaining olive oil over medium heat. Add the roasted garlic and red pepper flakes, and sauté for 1 minute.
5. Add the fresh spinach to the skillet and cook until wilted, about 2 minutes.
6. Stir in the cooked spaghetti, Parmesan cheese, salt, and black pepper. Toss to combine.
7. Serve hot.

Nutritional Information (per serving):
Calories: 380 | Protein: 10g | Carbohydrates: 45g | Fats: 18g | Fiber: 5g | Cholesterol: 10mg | Sodium: 300mg

Health Benefits: Roasted Garlic and Spinach Pasta is a delicious and healthy dish rich in antioxidants and fiber, promoting digestive health and overall wellness. The combination of roasted garlic, spinach, and olive oil provides essential vitamins and minerals, aligning with the Mediterranean Diet's emphasis on fresh, nutritious ingredients.

Mediterranean Pasta Primavera

Serves:4 | Prep Time:10 min | Cook Time:15 min

- 8 oz penne pasta
- 2 tbsp olive oil
- 1 small zucchini, diced
- 1 red bell pepper, diced
- 1 yellow bell pepper, diced
- 1 cup cherry tomatoes, halved
- 2 cloves garlic, minced
- 1/2 cup Kalamata olives, pitted and halved
- 1/4 cup crumbled feta cheese
- 1/4 cup fresh basil, chopped
- 1 tsp dried oregano
- 1/2 tsp salt
- 1/4 tsp black pepper

1. Cook the penne pasta according to package instructions. Drain and set aside.
2. In a large skillet, heat the olive oil over medium heat. Add the zucchini, red bell pepper, and yellow bell pepper. Cook for 5 minutes, stirring occasionally.
3. Add the cherry tomatoes, garlic, and Kalamata olives to the skillet. Cook for another 2 minutes.
4. Stir in the cooked penne, feta cheese, basil, oregano, salt, and black pepper. Toss to combine.
5. Serve hot.

Nutritional Information (per serving): Calories: 350 | Protein: 10g | Carbohydrates: 50g | Fats: 14g | Fiber: 6g | Cholesterol: 10mg | Sodium: 450mg

Health Benefits: Mediterranean Pasta Primavera is a nutritious and flavorful dish rich in fiber and antioxidants, promoting overall health and immune function. The combination of fresh vegetables, penne, and feta provides essential vitamins and minerals, aligning with the Mediterranean Diet's emphasis on fresh, nutritious ingredients.

Greek-Style Lasagna

Serves:6 | Prep Time:10 min | Cook Time:20 min

- 9 pre-cooked lasagna noodles
- 1 lb ground lamb or beef
- 1 onion, chopped
- 2 cloves garlic, minced
- 1 can (14 oz) diced tomatoes
- 1 tsp dried oregano
- 1/2 tsp ground cinnamon
- 1/2 tsp salt
- 1/4 tsp black pepper
- 2 cups ricotta cheese
- 1 cup crumbled feta cheese
- 1/2 cup grated Parmesan cheese
- 1 egg, beaten
- 2 cups marinara sauce

1. Preheat your oven to 375°F (190°C). Grease a baking dish with olive oil.
2, In a large skillet, cook the ground lamb or beef over medium heat until browned. Add the onion and garlic, and cook until softened, about 3-5 minutes.
3. Stir in the diced tomatoes, oregano, cinnamon, salt, and black pepper. Simmer for 5 minutes.
4. In a large bowl, combine the ricotta cheese, feta cheese, Parmesan cheese, and beaten egg.
5. Spread a thin layer of marinara sauce on the bottom of the prepared baking dish. Layer 3 lasagna noodles on top. Spread 1/3 of the meat mixture over the noodles, followed by 1/3 of the cheese mixture. Repeat the layers twice, ending with a layer of marinara sauce.
6. Cover the baking dish with foil and bake in the preheated oven for 20 minutes. Remove the foil and bake for an additional 5 minutes, or until the cheese is melted and bubbly.
7. Let the lasagna cool for 5 minutes before serving.

Nutritional Information (per serving): Calories: 450 | Protein: 25g | Carbohydrates: 40g | Fats: 22g | Fiber: 4g | Cholesterol: 80mg | Sodium: 800mg

Health Benefits: Greek-Style Lasagna is a hearty and flavorful dish rich in protein and antioxidants, promoting muscle health and overall wellness. The combination of ground lamb or beef, ricotta, and feta provides essential vitamins and minerals, aligning with the Mediterranean Diet's emphasis on fresh, nutritious ingredients.

Lemon Dill Salmon Pasta

Serves:4 | Prep Time:10 min | Cook Time:15 min

- 8 oz spaghetti
- 2 tbsp olive oil
- 2 cloves garlic, minced
- 1 lb salmon fillets, skin removed and cut into bite-sized pieces
- 1/4 cup fresh lemon juice
- 1/4 cup fresh dill, chopped
- 1/2 cup heavy cream
- 1/2 cup grated Parmesan cheese
- 1/2 tsp salt
- 1/4 tsp black pepper
- Lemon zest (for garnish)

1. Cook the spaghetti according to package instructions. Drain and set aside.
2. In a large skillet, heat the olive oil over medium heat. Add the garlic and sauté until fragrant, about 1 minute.
3. Add the salmon pieces to the skillet and cook until opaque, about 4-5 minutes.
4. Stir in the lemon juice, fresh dill, heavy cream, Parmesan cheese, salt, and black pepper. Cook for another 2 minutes, stirring until the sauce thickens.
5. Add the cooked spaghetti to the skillet and toss to combine.
6. Garnish with lemon zest before serving.

Nutritional Information (per serving): Calories: 450 | Protein: 25g | Carbohydrates: 45g | Fats: 22g | Fiber: 3g | Cholesterol: 90mg | Sodium: 500mg

Health Benefits: Lemon Dill Salmon Pasta is a light and flavorful dish rich in omega-3 fatty acids and antioxidants, promoting heart health and overall wellness. The combination of salmon, dill, and lemon provides essential vitamins and minerals, aligning with the Mediterranean Diet's emphasis on fresh, nutritious ingredients.

Spaghetti with Olive Tapenade

Serves:4 | Prep Time:10 min | Cook Time:10 min

- 8 oz spaghetti
- 1/2 cup pitted Kalamata olives
- 1/4 cup pitted green olives
- 2 cloves garlic, minced
- 2 tbsp capers, drained
- 2 tbsp fresh parsley, chopped
- 2 tbsp lemon juice
- 1/4 cup extra-virgin olive oil
- 1/2 tsp red pepper flakes (optional)
- 1/4 cup grated Parmesan cheese
- 1/4 tsp salt
- 1/4 tsp black pepper

1. Cook the spaghetti according to package instructions. Drain and set aside.
2. In a food processor, combine the Kalamata olives, green olives, garlic, capers, parsley, lemon juice, and olive oil. Pulse until finely chopped and well combined.
3. In a large skillet, heat the olive tapenade over medium heat. Stir in the red pepper flakes, salt, and black pepper.
4. Add the cooked spaghetti to the skillet and toss to coat with the tapenade.
5. Serve hot, topped with grated Parmesan cheese.

Nutritional Information (per serving): Calories: 400 | Protein: 10g | Carbohydrates: 45g | Fats: 20g | Fiber: 4g | Cholesterol: 10mg | Sodium: 600mg

Health Benefits: Spaghetti with Olive Tapenade is a savory and healthy dish rich in healthy fats and antioxidants, promoting heart health and overall wellness. The combination of olives, capers, and olive oil provides essential vitamins and minerals, aligning with the Mediterranean Diet's emphasis on fresh, nutritious ingredients.

Mediterranean Mac and Cheese

Serves:4 | Prep Time:10 min | Cook Time:20 min

- 8 oz elbow macaroni
- 2 tbsp olive oil
- 2 cloves garlic, minced
- 1/4 cup sun-dried tomatoes, chopped
- 1/4 cup Kalamata olives, pitted and halved
- 1/4 cup crumbled feta cheese
- 1 cup milk
- 1/2 cup heavy cream
- 1 cup shredded mozzarella cheese
- 1/2 cup grated Parmesan cheese
- 1/2 tsp dried oregano
- 1/2 tsp salt
- 1/4 tsp black pepper
- Fresh basil, chopped (for garnish)

1. Cook the elbow macaroni according to package instructions. Drain and set aside.
2. In a large skillet, heat the olive oil over medium heat. Add the garlic and sauté until fragrant, about 1 minute.
3. Stir in the sun-dried tomatoes and Kalamata olives. Cook for another 2 minutes.
4. Add the milk and heavy cream to the skillet and bring to a simmer. Stir in the mozzarella cheese, Parmesan cheese, oregano, salt, and black pepper until the cheese is melted and the sauce is smooth.
5. Add the cooked macaroni to the skillet and toss to combine.
6. Stir in the crumbled feta cheese.
7. Serve hot, garnished with fresh basil.

Nutritional Information (per serving): Calories: 500 | Protein: 18g | Carbohydrates: 45g | Fats: 28g | Fiber: 3g | Cholesterol: 90mg | Sodium: 700mg

Health Benefits: Mediterranean Mac and Cheese is a creamy and savory dish rich in protein and healthy fats, promoting muscle health and overall wellness. The combination of sun-dried tomatoes, olives, and feta provides essential vitamins and minerals, aligning with the Mediterranean Diet's emphasis on fresh, nutritious ingredients.

CHAPTER 12

PIZZA, WRAPS, AND SANDWICHES - MEDITERRANEAN-STYLE COMFORT FOODS

Greek Chicken Wrap

Serves:4 | Prep Time:15 min | Cook Time:10 min

- 2 boneless, skinless chicken breasts
- 1 tbsp olive oil
- 1 tsp dried oregano
- 1/2 tsp salt
- 1/4 tsp black pepper
- 4 whole wheat wraps
- 1 cup hummus
- 1 cup cucumber, sliced
- 1 cup cherry tomatoes, halved
- 1/4 cup red onion, thinly sliced
- 1/2 cup crumbled feta cheese
- 1/4 cup Kalamata olives, pitted and halved
- Fresh parsley, chopped (for garnish)

1. Heat the olive oil in a large skillet over medium heat. Season the chicken breasts with oregano, salt, and black pepper. Cook the chicken for 5-7 minutes on each side, or until fully cooked. Let cool slightly, then slice into strips.
2. Spread 1/4 cup of hummus on each whole wheat wrap.
3. Divide the sliced chicken, cucumber, cherry tomatoes, red onion, feta cheese, and Kalamata olives evenly among the wraps.
4. Roll up the wraps tightly and slice in half.
5. Garnish with fresh parsley before serving.

Nutritional Information (per serving): Calories: 350 | Protein: 30g | Carbohydrates: 30g | Fats: 14g | Fiber: 6g | Cholesterol: 60mg | Sodium: 700mg

Health Benefits: Greek Chicken Wrap is a healthy and balanced meal rich in protein, healthy fats, and fiber, promoting muscle health and digestive wellness. The combination of chicken, fresh vegetables, and whole wheat wraps provides essential vitamins and minerals, aligning with the Mediterranean Diet's emphasis on fresh, nutritious ingredients.

Mediterranean Veggie Pizza

Serves:4 | Prep Time:15 min | Cook Time:15 min

- 1 pre-made pizza crust
- 1/2 cup tomato sauce
- 1 cup shredded mozzarella cheese
- 1/2 cup artichoke hearts, drained and chopped
- 1/2 cup roasted red peppers, sliced
- 1/4 cup Kalamata olives, pitted and halved
- 1/4 cup red onion, thinly sliced
- 1/4 cup crumbled feta cheese
- 1 tsp dried oregano
- Fresh basil, chopped (for garnish)

1. Preheat your oven to 450°F (230°C).
2. Place the pre-made pizza crust on a baking sheet.
3. Spread the tomato sauce evenly over the pizza crust.
4. Sprinkle the shredded mozzarella cheese over the sauce.
5. Top with artichoke hearts, roasted red peppers, Kalamata olives, red onion, and crumbled feta cheese.
6. Sprinkle dried oregano over the toppings.
7. Bake in the preheated oven for 12-15 minutes, or until the cheese is melted and bubbly.
8. Garnish with fresh basil before serving.

Nutritional Information (per serving): Calories: 300 | Protein: 12g | Carbohydrates: 35g | Fats: 14g | Fiber: 4g | Cholesterol: 30mg | Sodium: 600mg

Health Benefits: Mediterranean Veggie Pizza is a delicious and nutritious meal rich in fiber and antioxidants, promoting overall health and immune function. The combination of fresh vegetables, tomato sauce, and whole grains provides essential vitamins and minerals, aligning with the Mediterranean Diet's emphasis on fresh, nutritious ingredients.

Hummus and Veggie Wrap

Serves:4 | Prep Time:10 min | Cook Time:0 min

- 4 whole wheat wraps
- 1 cup hummus
- 1 cup cucumber, sliced
- 1 cup cherry tomatoes, halved
- 1/2 cup shredded carrots
- 1/2 cup red bell pepper, sliced
- 1/4 cup red onion, thinly sliced
- 1/4 cup crumbled feta cheese
- Fresh parsley, chopped (for garnish)

1. Spread 1/4 cup of hummus on each whole wheat wrap.
2. Divide the cucumber, cherry tomatoes, shredded carrots, red bell pepper, red onion, and crumbled feta cheese evenly among the wraps.
3. Roll up the wraps tightly and slice in half.
4. Garnish with fresh parsley before serving.

Nutritional Information (per serving): Calories: 280 | Protein: 10g | Carbohydrates: 35g | Fats: 12g | Fiber: 8g | Cholesterol: 10mg | Sodium: 450mg

Health Benefits: Hummus and Veggie Wrap is a fresh and healthy meal rich in fiber and antioxidants, promoting digestive health and overall wellness. The combination of hummus, fresh vegetables, and whole wheat wraps provides essential vitamins and minerals, aligning with the Mediterranean Diet's emphasis on fresh, nutritious ingredients.

Spinach and Feta Quesadilla

Serves:4 | Prep Time:10 min | Cook Time:10 min

- 4 whole wheat tortillas
- 2 cups fresh spinach, chopped
- 1 cup crumbled feta cheese
- 1/2 cup shredded mozzarella cheese
- 1/4 cup sun-dried tomatoes, chopped
- 1 tbsp olive oil
- Fresh parsley, chopped (for garnish)

1. Heat 1/2 tablespoon of olive oil in a large skillet over medium heat.
2. Place one tortilla in the skillet and sprinkle with 1/2 cup of chopped spinach, 1/4 cup of crumbled feta cheese, 1/4 cup of shredded mozzarella cheese, and 1 tablespoon of chopped sun-dried tomatoes.
3. Place another tortilla on top and press down gently.
4. Cook for 2-3 minutes on each side, or until the cheese is melted and the tortilla is golden brown.
5. Repeat with the remaining tortillas and filling.
6. Cut each quesadilla into wedges and garnish with fresh parsley before serving.

Nutritional Information (per serving): Calories: 320 | Protein: 12g | Carbohydrates: 30g | Fats: 18g | Fiber: 4g | Cholesterol: 25mg | Sodium: 500mg

Health Benefits: Spinach and Feta Quesadilla is a delicious and nutritious meal rich in antioxidants and healthy fats, promoting heart health and overall wellness. The combination of spinach, feta, and sun-dried tomatoes provides essential vitamins and minerals, aligning with the Mediterranean Diet's emphasis on fresh, nutritious ingredients.

Pesto and Tomato Flatbread

Serves:4 | Prep Time:10 min | Cook Time:10 min

- 2 pre-made flatbreads
- 1/2 cup basil pesto
- 1 cup cherry tomatoes, halved
- 1/2 cup mozzarella cheese, shredded
- 1/4 cup crumbled feta cheese
- Fresh basil leaves (for garnish)
- 1 tbsp olive oil

1. Preheat your oven to 400°F (200°C).
2. Place the flatbreads on a baking sheet.
3. Spread 1/4 cup of basil pesto on each flatbread.
4. Top with cherry tomatoes, mozzarella cheese, and crumbled feta cheese.
5. Drizzle with olive oil.
6. Bake in the preheated oven for 10 minutes, or until the cheese is melted and bubbly.
7. Garnish with fresh basil leaves before serving.

Nutritional Information (per serving): Calories: 300 | Protein: 10g | Carbohydrates: 30g | Fats: 16g | Fiber: 2g | Cholesterol: 20mg | Sodium: 450mg

Health Benefits: Pesto and Tomato Flatbread is a delicious and healthy meal rich in antioxidants and healthy fats, promoting heart health and overall wellness. The combination of pesto, tomatoes, and cheeses provides essential vitamins and minerals, aligning with the Mediterranean Diet's emphasis on fresh, nutritious ingredients.

Mediterranean Tuna Salad Sandwich

Serves:4 | Prep Time:10 min | Cook Time:0 min

- 2 cans (5 oz each) tuna in water, drained
- 1/4 cup mayonnaise
- 1/4 cup plain Greek yogurt
- 1 tbsp lemon juice
- 1/4 cup Kalamata olives, pitted and chopped
- 1/4 cup red onion, finely chopped
- 1/4 cup celery, finely chopped
- 1 tbsp fresh parsley, chopped
- 1/2 tsp dried oregano
- Salt and black pepper to taste
- 8 slices whole grain bread
- 1 cup mixed greens

1. In a large bowl, combine the tuna, mayonnaise, Greek yogurt, lemon juice, Kalamata olives, red onion, celery, parsley, oregano, salt, and black pepper. Mix until well combined.
2. Spread the tuna salad evenly over 4 slices of bread.
3. Top with mixed greens and cover with the remaining slices of bread.
4. Serve immediately.

Nutritional Information (per serving): Calories: 300 | Protein: 20g | Carbohydrates: 30g | Fats: 12g | Fiber: 4g | Cholesterol: 35mg | Sodium: 550mg

Health Benefits: Mediterranean Tuna Salad Sandwich is a nutritious and satisfying meal rich in protein and healthy fats, promoting muscle health and heart wellness. The combination of tuna, olives, and whole grain bread provides essential vitamins and minerals, aligning with the Mediterranean Diet's emphasis on fresh, nutritious ingredients.

Chicken and Olive Pita

Serves:4 | Prep Time:15 min | Cook Time:10 min

- 2 boneless, skinless chicken breasts
- 1 tbsp olive oil
- 1 tsp dried oregano
- 1/2 tsp salt
- 1/4 tsp black pepper
- 4 whole wheat pitas
- 1 cup hummus
- 1/2 cup Kalamata olives, pitted and sliced
- 1/2 cup cucumber, sliced
- 1/2 cup cherry tomatoes, halved
- 1/4 cup red onion, thinly sliced
- Fresh parsley, chopped (for garnish)

1. Heat the olive oil in a large skillet over medium heat. Season the chicken breasts with oregano, salt, and black pepper. Cook the chicken for 5-7 minutes on each side, or until fully cooked. Let cool slightly, then slice into strips.
2. Warm the pitas in the oven or microwave.
3. Spread 1/4 cup of hummus inside each pita.
4. Divide the sliced chicken, Kalamata olives, cucumber, cherry tomatoes, and red onion evenly among the pitas.
5. Garnish with fresh parsley before serving.

Nutritional Information (per serving): Calories: 350 | Protein: 30g | Carbohydrates: 35g | Fats: 12g | Fiber: 6g | Cholesterol: 60mg | Sodium: 700mg

Health Benefits: Chicken and Olive Pita is a healthy and balanced meal rich in protein, healthy fats, and fiber, promoting muscle health and digestive wellness. The combination of chicken, fresh vegetables, and whole wheat pitas provides essential vitamins and minerals, aligning with the Mediterranean Diet's emphasis on fresh, nutritious ingredients.

Roasted Vegetable Panini

Serves:4 | Prep Time:10 min | Cook Time:15 min

- 1 red bell pepper, sliced
- 1 yellow bell pepper, sliced
- 1 zucchini, sliced
- 1 red onion, sliced
- 2 tbsp olive oil
- 1/2 tsp salt
- 1/4 tsp black pepper
- 4 ciabatta rolls, halved
- 1/2 cup hummus
- 1/2 cup crumbled feta cheese
- Fresh basil leaves (for garnish)

1. Preheat your oven to 400°F (200°C).
2. Place the bell peppers, zucchini, and red onion on a baking sheet. Drizzle with olive oil and season with salt and black pepper. Roast in the preheated oven for 15 minutes, or until the vegetables are tender.
3. Spread 2 tablespoons of hummus on each ciabatta roll half.
4. Layer the roasted vegetables and crumbled feta cheese on the bottom halves of the ciabatta rolls. Top with fresh basil leaves.
5. Cover with the top halves of the ciabatta rolls and press down gently.
6. Heat a panini press or grill pan over medium heat. Grill the paninis for 3-5 minutes on each side, or until the bread is golden brown and crispy. Serve hot.

Nutritional Information (per serving): Calories: 350 | Protein: 10g | Carbohydrates: 45g | Fats: 16g | Fiber: 6g | Cholesterol: 20mg | Sodium: 600mg

Health Benefits: The combination of roasted vegetables, hummus, and whole grains provides essential vitamins and minerals, aligning with the Mediterranean Diet's emphasis on fresh, nutritious

Greek-Style Gyro

Serves:4 | Prep Time:15 min | Cook Time:10 min

- 1 lb ground lamb or beef
- 1 tsp dried oregano
- 1 tsp ground cumin
- 1/2 tsp garlic powder
- 1/2 tsp onion powder
- 1/2 tsp salt
- 1/4 tsp black pepper
- 4 pita breads
- 1 cup tzatziki sauce
- 1 cup lettuce, shredded
- 1 cup cherry tomatoes, halved
- 1/4 cup red onion, thinly sliced
- Fresh parsley, chopped (for garnish)

1. In a large bowl, combine the ground lamb or beef, oregano, cumin, garlic powder, onion powder, salt, and black pepper. Mix until well combined.
2. Heat a large skillet over medium heat. Add the meat mixture and cook, breaking it up with a spoon, until browned and fully cooked, about 8-10 minutes. Drain any excess fat.
3. Warm the pita breads in the oven or microwave.
4. Spread 1/4 cup of tzatziki sauce on each pita bread.
5. Divide the cooked meat, lettuce, cherry tomatoes, and red onion evenly among the pitas.
6. Garnish with fresh parsley before serving.

Nutritional Information (per serving): Calories: 400 | Protein: 25g | Carbohydrates: 35g | Fats: 18g | Fiber: 4g | Cholesterol: 70mg | Sodium: 600mg

Health Benefits: It is a flavorful and nutritious meal rich in protein and healthy fats, promoting muscle health and overall wellness. The combination of ground meat, fresh vegetables, and whole wheat pita provides essential vitamins and minerals, aligning with the Mediterranean Diet's emphasis on fresh, nutritious ingredients.

Spicy Falafel Wrap

Serves:4 | Prep Time:15 min | Cook Time:10 min

- 2 cups cooked chickpeas
- 1 small onion, chopped
- 2 cloves garlic, minced
- 1/4 cup fresh parsley, chopped
- 1 tsp ground cumin
- 1 tsp ground coriander
- 1/2 tsp ground cayenne pepper
- 1/2 tsp salt
- 1/4 tsp black pepper
- 2 tbsp flour
- 2 tbsp olive oil
- 4 whole wheat wraps
- 1 cup hummus

- 1 cup lettuce, shredded
- 1 cup cucumber, sliced
- 1/2 cup cherry tomatoes, halved
- Fresh cilantro, chopped (for garnish)

1. In a food processor, combine the chickpeas, onion, garlic, parsley, cumin, coriander, cayenne pepper, salt, black pepper, and flour. Pulse until the mixture is well combined and slightly chunky.
2. Form the mixture into small patties.
3. Heat the olive oil in a large skillet over medium heat. Cook the falafel patties for 3-4 minutes on each side, or until golden brown and crispy.
4. Warm the whole wheat wraps in the oven or microwave.
5. Spread 1/4 cup of hummus on each wrap.
6. Divide the falafel patties, lettuce, cucumber, and cherry tomatoes evenly among the wraps.
7. Garnish with fresh cilantro before serving.

Nutritional Information (per serving): Calories: 350 | Protein: 12g | Carbohydrates: 45g | Fats: 14g | Fiber: 8g | Cholesterol: 0mg | Sodium: 500mg

Health Benefits: It is a delicious and healthy meal rich in fiber and plant-based protein, promoting digestive health and overall wellness. The combination of chickpeas, fresh vegetables, and whole wheat wraps provides essential vitamins and minerals.

Mediterranean Turkey Burger

Serves:4 | Prep Time:15 min | Cook Time:10 min

- 1 lb ground turkey
- 1/4 cup red onion, finely chopped
- 1/4 cup Kalamata olives, pitted and chopped
- 1/4 cup feta cheese, crumbled
- 2 tbsp fresh parsley, chopped
- 1 tsp dried oregano
- 1/2 tsp salt
- 1/4 tsp black pepper
- 4 whole wheat burger buns
- 1 cup mixed greens
- 1/2 cup tzatziki sauce

1. In a large bowl, combine the ground turkey, red onion, Kalamata olives, feta cheese, parsley, oregano, salt, and black pepper. Mix until well combined.
2. Form the mixture into 4 patties.
3. Heat a grill or skillet over medium heat. Cook the turkey patties for 5-6 minutes on each side, or until fully cooked.
4. Toast the whole wheat burger buns.
5. Place a turkey patty on each bun and top with mixed greens and a dollop of tzatziki sauce.

Nutritional Information (per serving): Calories: 400 | Protein: 30g | Carbohydrates: 30g | Fats: 18g | Fiber: 5g | Cholesterol: 70mg | Sodium: 700mg

Health Benefits: Mediterranean Turkey Burger is a healthy and flavorful meal rich in protein and healthy fats, promoting muscle health and overall wellness. The combination of ground turkey, fresh vegetables, and whole wheat buns provides essential vitamins and minerals, aligning with the Mediterranean Diet's emphasis on fresh, nutritious ingredients.

Grilled Halloumi Sandwich

Serves:4 | Prep Time:10 min | Cook Time:10 min

- 8 oz halloumi cheese, sliced
- 1 tbsp olive oil
- 4 whole wheat sandwich rolls
- 1/2 cup hummus
- 1 cup arugula
- 1/2 cup roasted red peppers, sliced
- 1/4 cup red onion, thinly sliced
- Fresh basil leaves (for garnish)

1. Heat the olive oil in a large skillet over medium heat.
2. Add the halloumi slices and cook for 2-3 minutes on each side, or until golden brown and crispy.
3. Slice the sandwich rolls in half and spread 2 tablespoons of hummus on each bottom half.
4. Layer the arugula, roasted red peppers, red onion, and grilled halloumi on the hummus.
5. Top with fresh basil leaves and cover with the top halves of the sandwich rolls.

Nutritional Information (per serving): Calories: 350 | Protein: 15g | Carbohydrates: 35g | Fats: 16g | Fiber: 4g | Cholesterol: 30mg | Sodium: 700mg

Health Benefits: Grilled Halloumi Sandwich is a delicious and nutritious meal rich in protein and healthy fats, promoting heart health and overall wellness. The combination of halloumi, fresh vegetables, and whole wheat rolls provides essential vitamins and minerals, aligning with the Mediterranean Diet's emphasis on fresh, nutritious ingredients.

Tomato Basil Mozzarella Sandwich

Serves:4 | Prep Time:10 min | Cook Time:0 min

- 8 slices whole grain bread
- 2 tbsp olive oil
- 2 large tomatoes, sliced
- 8 oz fresh mozzarella, sliced
- 1/4 cup fresh basil leaves
- 2 tbsp balsamic glaze
- Salt and black pepper to taste

1. Drizzle olive oil on one side of each slice of bread.
2. Layer tomato slices, mozzarella slices, and fresh basil leaves on 4 slices of bread (on the non-oiled side).
3. Drizzle with balsamic glaze and season with salt and black pepper.
4. Top with the remaining slices of bread (olive oil side up).

Nutritional Information (per serving): Calories: 350 | Protein: 15g | Carbohydrates: 30g | Fats: 20g | Fiber: 4g | Cholesterol: 30mg | Sodium: 400mg

Health Benefits: Tomato Basil Mozzarella Sandwich is a fresh and nutritious meal rich in antioxidants and healthy fats, promoting heart health and overall wellness. The combination of tomatoes, mozzarella, and basil provides essential vitamins and minerals, aligning with the Mediterranean Diet's emphasis on fresh, nutritious ingredients.

Spicy Chicken Pita

Serves:4 | Prep Time:15 min | Cook Time:10 min

- 2 boneless, skinless chicken breasts
- 1 tbsp olive oil
- 1 tsp ground cumin
- 1/2 tsp ground paprika
- 1/2 tsp garlic powder
- 1/2 tsp salt
- 1/4 tsp black pepper
- 4 whole wheat pitas
- 1 cup hummus
- 1 cup shredded lettuce
- 1/2 cup cucumber, sliced
- 1/2 cup cherry tomatoes, halved
- Fresh cilantro, chopped (for garnish)

1. In a small bowl, mix the cumin, paprika, garlic powder, salt, and black pepper. Rub the spice mixture onto the chicken breasts.
2. Heat the olive oil in a large skillet over medium heat. Cook the chicken breasts for 5-7 minutes on each side, or until fully cooked. Let cool slightly, then slice into strips.
3. Warm the pitas in the oven or microwave.
4. Spread 1/4 cup of hummus inside each pita.
5. Divide the sliced chicken, lettuce, cucumber, and cherry tomatoes evenly among the pitas.
6. Garnish with fresh cilantro before serving.

Nutritional Information (per serving): Calories: 350 | Protein: 30g | Carbohydrates: 35g | Fats: 12g | Fiber: 6g | Cholesterol: 60mg | Sodium: 700mg

Health Benefits: It is a flavorful and balanced meal rich in protein, healthy fats, and fiber, promoting muscle health and digestive wellness. The combination of spiced chicken, fresh vegetables, and whole wheat pitas provides essential vitamins and minerals.

Mediterranean Shrimp Tacos

Serves:4 | Prep Time:15 min | Cook Time:10 min

- 1 lb shrimp, peeled and deveined
- 1 tbsp olive oil
- 1 tsp ground cumin
- 1/2 tsp smoked paprika
- 1/2 tsp garlic powder
- 1/2 tsp salt
- 1/4 tsp black pepper
- 8 small whole wheat tortillas
- 1 cup shredded lettuce
- 1/2 cup cherry tomatoes, halved
- 1/2 cup red onion, thinly sliced
- 1/4 cup crumbled feta cheese
- 1/4 cup tzatziki sauce
- Fresh parsley, chopped (for garnish)

1. In a small bowl, mix the cumin, smoked paprika, garlic powder, salt, and black pepper. Rub the spice mixture onto the shrimp.
2. Heat the olive oil in a large skillet over medium heat. Cook the shrimp for 2-3 minutes on each side, or until pink and fully cooked.
3. Warm the tortillas in the oven or microwave.
4. Divide the shrimp, lettuce, cherry tomatoes, red onion, and feta cheese evenly among the tortillas.
5. Drizzle with tzatziki sauce and garnish with fresh parsley before serving.

Nutritional Information (per serving): Calories: 300 | Protein: 20g | Carbohydrates: 30g | Fats: 12g | Fiber: 4g | Cholesterol: 120mg | Sodium: 600mg

Health Benefits: Mediterranean Shrimp Tacos are a delicious and healthy meal rich in protein and antioxidants, promoting muscle health and overall wellness. The combination of spiced shrimp, fresh vegetables, and whole wheat tortillas provides essential vitamins and minerals, aligning with the Mediterranean Diet's emphasis on fresh, nutritious ingredients.

CHAPTER 13

STAPLES, SAUCES, DIPS, AND DRESSINGS – ESSENTIAL ADDITIONS TO YOUR MEALS

Classic Tzatziki Sauce

Serves:6 | Prep Time:10 min | Cook Time:0 min

- 1 cup plain Greek yogurt
- 1 cucumber, grated and excess water squeezed out
- 2 cloves garlic, minced
- 1 tbsp olive oil
- 1 tbsp lemon juice
- 1 tbsp fresh dill, chopped
- 1/2 tsp salt
- 1/4 tsp black pepper

1. In a medium bowl, combine the Greek yogurt, grated cucumber, garlic, olive oil, lemon juice, dill, salt, and black pepper.
2. Mix until well combined.
3. Refrigerate for at least 30 minutes before serving to allow the flavors to meld.
4. Serve as a dip or sauce.

Nutritional Information (per serving): Calories: 50 | Protein: 4g | Carbohydrates: 3g | Fats: 3g | Fiber: 0g | Cholesterol: 5mg | Sodium: 200mg

Health Benefits: Classic Tzatziki Sauce is a light and refreshing dip rich in protein and probiotics, promoting digestive health and overall wellness.

Lemon Herb Vinaigrette

Serves:6 | Prep Time:5 min | Cook Time:0 min

- 1/4 cup olive oil
- 2 tbsp lemon juice
- 1 tbsp red wine vinegar
- 1 tsp Dijon mustard
- 1 clove garlic, minced
- 1 tbsp fresh parsley, chopped
- 1 tbsp fresh basil, chopped
- 1/2 tsp salt
- 1/4 tsp black pepper

1. In a small bowl, whisk together the olive oil, lemon juice, red wine vinegar, Dijon mustard, and garlic.
2. Stir in the parsley, basil, salt, and black pepper.
3. Mix until well combined. Refrigerate until ready to use. Shake well before serving.

Nutritional Information (per serving): Calories: 70 | Protein: 0g | Carbohydrates: 1g | Fats: 7g | Fiber: 0g | Cholesterol: 0mg | Sodium: 100mg

Health Benefits: Lemon Herb Vinaigrette is a flavorful and healthy dressing rich in healthy fats and antioxidants, promoting heart health and overall wellness. The combination of olive oil, lemon juice, and fresh herbs provides essential vitamins and minerals, aligning with the Mediterranean Diet's emphasis on fresh, nutritious ingredients.

Roasted Red Pepper Hummus

Serves:6 | Prep Time:10 min | Cook Time:0 min

- 1 can (15 oz) chickpeas, drained and rinsed
- 1 roasted red bell pepper, chopped
- 2 tbsp tahini
- 2 tbsp lemon juice
- 2 cloves garlic, minced
- 2 tbsp olive oil
- 1/2 tsp cumin
- 1/2 tsp salt
- 1/4 tsp smoked paprika
- 2-3 tbsp water (as needed)

1. In a food processor, combine the chickpeas, roasted red bell pepper, tahini, lemon juice, garlic, olive oil, cumin, salt, and smoked paprika.
2. Blend until smooth, adding water as needed to reach desired consistency.
3. Serve as a dip with vegetables, pita bread, or as a spread.

Nutritional Information (per serving): Calories: 100 | Protein: 3g | Carbohydrates: 10g | Fats: 6g | Fiber: 3g | Cholesterol: 0mg | Sodium: 200mg

Health Benefits: Roasted Red Pepper Hummus is a nutritious and delicious dip rich in fiber and plant-based protein, promoting digestive health and overall wellness.

Garlic and Herb Pesto

Serves:6 | Prep Time:10 min | Cook Time:0 min

- 2 cups fresh basil leaves
- 1/2 cup fresh parsley
- 3 cloves garlic
- 1/4 cup pine nuts
- 1/2 cup grated Parmesan cheese
- 1/2 cup olive oil
- 1 tbsp lemon juice
- Salt and black pepper to taste

1. In a food processor, combine the basil, parsley, garlic, pine nuts, and Parmesan cheese. Pulse until finely chopped.
2. With the processor running, slowly add the olive oil and lemon juice until the mixture is smooth.
3. Season with salt and black pepper to taste.

Nutritional Information (per serving): Calories: 180 | Protein: 4g | Carbohydrates: 3g | Fats: 18g | Fiber: 1g | Cholesterol: 5mg | Sodium: 150mg

Health Benefits: Garlic and Herb Pesto is a flavorful and nutritious sauce rich in antioxidants and healthy fats, promoting heart health and overall wellness. The combination of fresh herbs, garlic, and olive oil provides essential vitamins and minerals, aligning with the Mediterranean Diet's emphasis on fresh, nutritious ingredients.

Spicy Harissa Paste

Serves:6 | Prep Time:10 min | Cook Time:0 min

- 2 red bell peppers, roasted and peeled
- 2 cloves garlic
- 1 tbsp ground cumin
- 1 tbsp ground coriander
- 1 tbsp smoked paprika
- 1 tsp cayenne pepper (adjust to taste)
- 2 tbsp tomato paste
- 2 tbsp olive oil
- 1 tbsp lemon juice
- Salt to taste

1. In a food processor, combine the roasted red bell peppers, garlic, cumin, coriander, smoked paprika, cayenne pepper, tomato paste, olive oil, and lemon juice.
2. Blend until smooth.
3. Season with salt to taste.
4. Serve immediately or store in an airtight container in the refrigerator.

Nutritional Information (per serving): Calories: 50 | Protein: 1g | Carbohydrates: 5g | Fats: 3g | Fiber: 1g | Cholesterol: 0mg | Sodium: 150mg

Health Benefits: It is a bold and spicy condiment rich in antioxidants and anti-inflammatory properties, promoting overall health and wellness.

Mediterranean Tapenade

Serves:6 | Prep Time:10 min | Cook Time:0 min

- 1 cup Kalamata olives, pitted
- 1/4 cup green olives, pitted
- 2 cloves garlic
- 2 tbsp capers, drained
- 2 tbsp fresh parsley
- 2 tbsp lemon juice
- 1/4 cup olive oil
- Salt and black pepper to taste

1. In a food processor, combine the Kalamata olives, green olives, garlic, capers, parsley, and lemon juice. Pulse until finely chopped.
2. With the processor running, slowly add the olive oil until the mixture is well combined but still slightly chunky.
3. Season with salt and black pepper to taste.
4. Serve immediately or store in an airtight container in the refrigerator.

Nutritional Information (per serving): Calories: 100 | Protein: 1g | Carbohydrates: 2g | Fats: 10g | Fiber: 1g | Cholesterol: 0mg | Sodium: 300mg

Health Benefits: Mediterranean Tapenade is a savory and healthy dip rich in healthy fats and antioxidants, promoting heart health and overall wellness. The combination of olives, capers, and olive oil provides essential vitamins and minerals, aligning with the Mediterranean Diet's emphasis on fresh, nutritious ingredients.

Lemon Dill Yogurt Sauce

Serves:6 | Prep Time:5 min | Cook Time:0 min

- 1 cup plain Greek yogurt
- 1 tbsp lemon juice
- 2 tsp lemon zest
- 2 tbsp fresh dill, chopped
- 1 clove garlic, minced
- Salt and black pepper to taste

1. In a medium bowl, combine the Greek yogurt, lemon juice, lemon zest, dill, and garlic.
2. Mix until well combined.
3. Season with salt and black pepper to taste.
4. Serve immediately or refrigerate until ready to use.

Nutritional Information (per serving): Calories: 40 | Protein: 4g | Carbohydrates: 3g | Fats: 1g | Fiber: 0g | Cholesterol: 5mg | Sodium: 100mg

Health Benefits: Lemon Dill Yogurt Sauce is a light and refreshing condiment rich in protein and probiotics, promoting digestive health and overall wellness.

Greek-Style Marinade

Serves:6 | Prep Time:5 min | Cook Time:0 min

- 1/2 cup olive oil
- 1/4 cup lemon juice
- 3 cloves garlic, minced
- 2 tbsp red wine vinegar
- 1 tbsp dried oregano
- 1 tbsp fresh parsley, chopped
- 1 tsp dried thyme
- 1/2 tsp salt
- 1/4 tsp black pepper

1. In a medium bowl, whisk together the olive oil, lemon juice, garlic, red wine vinegar, oregano, parsley, thyme, salt, and black pepper.
2. Use immediately to marinate meats, fish, or vegetables, or store in an airtight container in the refrigerator for up to one week.

Nutritional Information (per serving): Calories: 100 | Protein: 0g | Carbohydrates: 1g | Fats: 10g | Fiber: 0g | Cholesterol: 0mg | Sodium: 100mg

Health Benefits: Greek-Style Marinade is a flavorful and healthy addition to any meal, rich in healthy fats and antioxidants.

Spicy Tomato Chutney

Serves:6 | Prep Time:10 min | Cook Time:20 min

- 4 ripe tomatoes, chopped
- 1 small onion, finely chopped
- 2 cloves garlic, minced
- 1 tbsp olive oil
- 1 tbsp red wine vinegar
- 1 tsp ground cumin
- 1/2 tsp ground coriander
- 1/2 tsp red pepper flakes (adjust to taste)
- 1/2 tsp salt
- 1/4 tsp black pepper
- 1 tbsp fresh cilantro, chopped

1. Heat the olive oil in a medium saucepan over medium heat.
2. Add the onion and garlic, and sauté until softened, about 5 minutes.
3. Stir in the tomatoes, red wine vinegar, cumin, coriander, red pepper flakes, salt, and black pepper.
4. Bring to a simmer and cook for 15-20 minutes, or until the chutney thickens.
5. Remove from heat and stir in the fresh cilantro.
6. Serve warm or cold, or store in an airtight container in the refrigerator.

Nutritional Information (per serving): Calories: 40 | Protein: 1g | Carbohydrates: 6g | Fats: 1g | Fiber: 1g | Cholesterol: 0mg | Sodium: 200mg

Health Benefits: Spicy Tomato Chutney is a delicious and nutritious condiment rich in antioxidants and anti-inflammatory properties. The combination of tomatoes, onions, and spices provides essential vitamins and minerals, aligning with the Mediterranean Diet's emphasis on fresh, nutritious ingredients.

Classic Hummus

Serves:6 | Prep Time:10 min | Cook Time:0 min

- 1 can (15 oz) chickpeas, drained and rinsed
- 1/4 cup tahini
- 2 tbsp lemon juice
- 2 cloves garlic, minced
- 2 tbsp olive oil
- 1/2 tsp ground cumin
- 1/2 tsp salt
- 2-3 tbsp water (as needed)
- Paprika and olive oil (for garnish)

1. In a food processor, combine the chickpeas, tahini, lemon juice, garlic, olive oil, cumin, and salt.
2. Blend until smooth, adding water as needed to reach the desired consistency.
3. Transfer to a serving bowl and drizzle with olive oil and sprinkle with paprika.
4. Serve with pita bread, vegetables, or as a spread.

Nutritional Information (per serving): Calories: 120 | Protein: 4g | Carbohydrates: 12g | Fats: 6g | Fiber: 4g | Cholesterol: 0mg | Sodium: 200mg

Health Benefits: Classic Hummus is a nutritious and delicious dip rich in fiber and plant-based protein, promoting digestive health and overall wellness. The combination of chickpeas, tahini, and olive oil provides essential vitamins and minerals, aligning with the Mediterranean Diet's emphasis on fresh, nutritious ingredients.

Roasted Garlic Aioli

Serves:6 | Prep Time:10 min | Cook Time:30 min

- 1 head garlic
- 1/2 cup mayonnaise
- 2 tbsp lemon juice
- 1 tbsp olive oil
- Salt and black pepper to taste

1. Preheat Oven: Preheat your oven to 400°F (200°C).
2. Roast Garlic: If not pre-roasted, cut the top off the head of garlic to expose the cloves. Drizzle with olive oil and wrap in aluminum foil. Roast in the preheated oven for 30 minutes, or until the garlic is soft and caramelized.
3. Prepare Garlic: Let the garlic cool slightly, then squeeze the roasted cloves out of their skins into a small bowl.
4. Combine Ingredients: In a medium bowl, combine the roasted garlic, mayonnaise, lemon juice, olive oil, salt, and black pepper.
5. Mix and Serve: Mix until smooth. Serve as a dip or spread, or store in an airtight container in the refrigerator.

Nutritional Information (per serving): Calories: 80 | Protein: 1g | Carbohydrates: 2g | Fats: 8g | Fiber: 0g | Cholesterol: 5mg | Sodium: 150mg

Health Benefits: It is a flavorful and creamy sauce rich in antioxidants and healthy fats, promoting heart health and overall wellness.

Lemon Garlic Dressing

Serves:6 | Prep Time:5 min | Cook Time:0 min

- 1/4 cup olive oil
- 2 tbsp lemon juice
- 1 tbsp red wine vinegar
- 2 cloves garlic, minced
- 1 tsp Dijon mustard
- 1/2 tsp salt
- 1/4 tsp black pepper

1. In a small bowl, whisk together the olive oil, lemon juice, red wine vinegar, garlic, Dijon mustard, salt, and black pepper until well combined.
2. Serve immediately or store in an airtight container in the refrigerator. Shake well before serving.

Nutritional Information (per serving): Calories: 70 | Protein: 0g | Carbohydrates: 1g | Fats: 7g | Fiber: 0g | Cholesterol: 0mg | Sodium: 100mg

Health Benefits: It is a light and refreshing dressing rich in healthy fats and antioxidants, promoting heart health and overall wellness.

Cucumber Mint Raita

Serves:6 | Prep Time:10 min | Cook Time:0 min

- 1 cup plain Greek yogurt
- 1 cucumber, grated and excess water squeezed out
- 1/4 cup fresh mint leaves, chopped
- 1 tbsp lemon juice
- 1 clove garlic, minced
- 1/2 tsp salt
- 1/4 tsp black pepper

1. In a medium bowl, combine the Greek yogurt, grated cucumber, mint leaves, lemon juice, garlic, salt, and black pepper.
2. Mix until well combined.
3. Refrigerate for at least 30 minutes before serving to allow the flavors to meld.
4. Serve as a dip or sauce.

Nutritional Information (per serving): Calories: 50 | Protein: 4g | Carbohydrates: 3g | Fats: 2g | Fiber: 0g | Cholesterol: 5mg | Sodium: 150mg

Health Benefits: Cucumber Mint Raita is a refreshing and healthy dip rich in protein and probiotics, promoting digestive health and overall wellness.

Smoky Eggplant Dip (Baba Ghanoush)

Serves:6 | Prep Time:10 min | Cook Time:30 min

- 1 large eggplant
- 1/4 cup tahini
- 2 tbsp lemon juice
- 2 cloves garlic, minced
- 2 tbsp olive oil
- 1/2 tsp ground cumin
- 1/2 tsp smoked paprika
- Salt to taste
- Fresh parsley, chopped (for garnish)

1. Preheat your oven to 400°F (200°C).
2. Prick the eggplant with a fork and place it on a baking sheet. Roast in the preheated oven for 30 minutes, or until the skin is charred and the flesh is soft.
3. Let the eggplant cool slightly, then scoop out the flesh and place it in a food processor.
4. Add the tahini, lemon juice, garlic, olive oil, cumin, smoked paprika, and salt. Blend until smooth.
5. Transfer to a serving bowl and garnish with fresh parsley.
6. Serve with pita bread or vegetables.

Nutritional Information (per serving): Calories: 80 | Protein: 2g | Carbohydrates: 6g | Fats: 6g | Fiber: 3g | Cholesterol: 0mg | Sodium: 100mg

Health Benefits: It is a nutritious and delicious dip rich in fiber and antioxidants, promoting digestive health and overall wellness.

Mediterranean Herb Blend

Serves:12 | Prep Time:5 min | Cook Time:0 min

- 2 tbsp dried oregano
- 2 tbsp dried basil
- 2 tbsp dried thyme
- 1 tbsp dried rosemary
- 1 tbsp dried marjoram
- 1 tbsp dried parsley
- 1 tsp garlic powder
- 1 tsp onion powder
- 1/2 tsp dried sage
- 1/2 tsp black pepper

1. In a small bowl, combine the dried oregano, basil, thyme, rosemary, marjoram, parsley, garlic powder, onion powder, sage, and black pepper.
2. Mix until well combined.
3. Store the herb blend in an airtight container in a cool, dry place.
4. Use as a seasoning for meats, vegetables, soups, and stews.

Nutritional Information (per serving): Calories: 2 | Protein: 0g | Carbohydrates: 0g | Fats: 0g | Fiber: 0g | Cholesterol: 0mg | Sodium: 0mg

Health Benefits: Mediterranean Herb Blend is a versatile and healthy seasoning rich in antioxidants and anti-inflammatory properties.

30-DAY MEDITERRANEAN MEAL PLAN

Days	Breakfast	Lunch	Dinner	Snack/Dessert
1	Greek Yogurt Parfait with Honey and Nuts	Mediterranean Shakshuka	Spinach and Feta Egg White Omelette	Olive Oil and Orange Muffins
2	Spinach and Feta Egg White Omelette	Quinoa Breakfast Bowl with Fresh Berries	Mediterranean Breakfast Burrito	Fig and Almond Oatmeal
3	Mediterranean Breakfast Burrito	Greek Salad with Feta	Pesto and Egg Breakfast Pizza	Greek Yogurt and Granola Parfait
4	Quinoa Breakfast Bowl with Fresh Berries	Sun-Dried Tomato and Spinach Frittata	Chickpea Flour Breakfast Crepes	Lemon Olive Oil Cake
5	Avocado and Tomato Toast	Hummus and Veggie Breakfast Wrap	Greek-Style Stuffed Peppers	Pistachio Baklava Bites
6	Smoked Salmon and Cucumber Bagel	Spinach and Strawberry Salad	Mediterranean Seafood Paella	Greek Yogurt with Honey and Walnuts
7	Lemon Ricotta Pancakes with Fresh Fruit	Roasted Beet and Goat Cheese Salad	Spinach and Feta Stuffed Peppers	Honey Poached Pears
8	Mediterranean Shakshuka	Tomato and Basil Bruschetta	Spaghetti Squash Primavera	Olive Oil and Citrus Cookies
9	Olive Oil and Orange Muffins	Chickpea and Cucumber Salad	Mediterranean Fish Stew	Chocolate-Dipped Figs
10	Fig and Almond Oatmeal	Greek-Style Gyro	Eggplant Parmesan	Spiced Honey Almonds
11	Hummus and Veggie Breakfast Wrap	Kale and Chickpea Salad	Lemon Dill Salmon Pasta	Lemon and Rosemary Shortbread
12	Pesto and Egg Breakfast Pizza	Watermelon and Feta Salad	Greek Beef Souvlaki	Grilled Halloumi with Lemon
13	Greek Yogurt and Granola Parfait	Tuna and White Bean Salad	Herb-Crusted Lamb Roast	Apricot and Almond Clafoutis
14	Sun-Dried Tomato and Spinach Frittata	Freekeh Salad with Pomegranate Seeds	Mediterranean Chicken Stew	Roasted Garlic and White Bean Dip
15	Chickpea Flour Breakfast Crepes	Bulgur Wheat Salad with Mint	Greek Chicken Gyro Wraps	Caprese Skewers
16	Greek Yogurt Parfait with Honey and Nuts	Mediterranean Shakshuka	Spinach and Feta Egg White Omelette	Olive Oil and Orange Muffins
17	Spinach and Feta Egg White Omelette	Quinoa Breakfast Bowl with Fresh Berries	Mediterranean Breakfast Burrito	Fig and Almond Oatmeal
18	Mediterranean Breakfast Burrito	Greek Salad with Feta	Pesto and Egg Breakfast Pizza	Greek Yogurt and Granola Parfait

30-DAY MEDITERRANEAN MEAL PLAN

Days	Breakfast	Lunch	Dinner	Snack/Dessert
19	Quinoa Breakfast Bowl with Fresh Berries	Sun-Dried Tomato and Spinach Frittata	Chickpea Flour Breakfast Crepes	Lemon Olive Oil Cake
20	Avocado and Tomato Toast	Hummus and Veggie Breakfast Wrap	Greek-Style Stuffed Peppers	Pistachio Baklava Bites
21	Smoked Salmon and Cucumber Bagel	Spinach and Strawberry Salad	Mediterranean Seafood Paella	Greek Yogurt with Honey and Walnuts
22	Lemon Ricotta Pancakes with Fresh Fruit	Roasted Beet and Goat Cheese Salad	Spinach and Feta Stuffed Peppers	Honey Poached Pears
23	Mediterranean Shakshuka	Tomato and Basil Bruschetta	Spaghetti Squash Primavera	Olive Oil and Citrus Cookies
24	Olive Oil and Orange Muffins	Chickpea and Cucumber Salad	Mediterranean Fish Stew	Chocolate-Dipped Figs
25	Fig and Almond Oatmeal	Greek-Style Gyro	Eggplant Parmesan	Spiced Honey Almonds
26	Hummus and Veggie Breakfast Wrap	Kale and Chickpea Salad	Lemon Dill Salmon Pasta	Lemon and Rosemary Shortbread
27	Pesto and Egg Breakfast Pizza	Watermelon and Feta Salad	Greek Beef Souvlaki	Grilled Halloumi with Lemon
28	Greek Yogurt and Granola Parfait	Tuna and White Bean Salad	Herb-Crusted Lamb Roast	Apricot and Almond Clafoutis
29	Sun-Dried Tomato and Spinach Frittata	Freekeh Salad with Pomegranate Seeds	Mediterranean Chicken Stew	Roasted Garlic and White Bean Dip
30	Chickpea Flour Breakfast Crepes	Bulgur Wheat Salad with Mint	Greek Chicken Gyro Wraps	Caprese Skewers

APPENDIX 1

MEASUREMENT CONVERSION CHART

LIQUIDS

US Customary	Metric	UK Imperial
1/8 teaspoon	0.625 milliliters (ml)	1/8 UK teaspoon
1/4 teaspoon	1.25 milliliters (ml)	1/4 UK teaspoon
1/2 teaspoon	2.5 milliliters (ml)	1/2 UK teaspoon
1 teaspoon (tsp)	5 milliliters (ml)	1 UK teaspoon
1 tablespoon (tbsp)	15 milliliters (ml)	1 UK tablespoon
1/4 cup	60 milliliters (ml)	1/4 UK cup
1/2 cup	120 milliliters (ml)	1/2 UK cup
3/4 cup	180 milliliters (ml)	3/4 UK cup
1 cup	240 milliliters (ml)	1 UK cup
2 cups	480 milliliters (ml)	2 UK cups
3 cups	720 milliliters (ml)	3 UK cups
1 fluid ounce (fl oz)	30 milliliters (ml)	1 UK fluid ounce (fl oz)

OVEN TEMPERATURES

Fahrenheit (°F)	Celsius (°C)
250°F	120°C
275°F	140°C
300°F	150°C
325°F	165°C
350°F	180°C
375°F	190°C
400°F	200°C
425°F	220°C
450°F	230°C
475°F	245°C
500°F	260°C

WEIGHTS

US Customary	Metric	UK Imperial
1 ounce (oz)	28 grams (g)	1 UK ounce (oz)
2 ounces (oz)	57 grams (g)	2 UK ounces (oz)
5 ounces (oz)	142 grams (g)	5 UK ounces (oz)
10 ounces (oz)	283 grams (g)	10 UK ounces (oz)
15 ounces (oz)	425 grams (g)	15 UK ounces (oz)
16 ounces (oz)	454 grams (g)	16 UK ounces (oz)
1 pound (lb)	454 grams (g)	1 UK pound (lb)
1.5 pounds (lb)	680 grams (g)	1.5 UK pounds (lb)

DRY INGREDIENTS

US Customary	Metric	UK Imperial
1 cup flour	120 grams (g)	1 UK cup flour
1 cup sugar	200 grams (g)	1 UK cup sugar
1 cup brown sugar	220 grams (g)	1 UK cup brown sugar
1 cup butter	227 grams (g)	1 UK cup butter

APPENDIX 2

THE DIRTY DOZEN AND CLEAN FIFTEEN

The Environmental Working Group (EWG) is a nonprofit organization focused on safeguarding human health and the environment. Their goal is to enable individuals to lead healthier lives in a healthier environment. Each year, EWG releases a list identifying the top twelve fruits and vegetables with the highest pesticide residues, known as the Dirty Dozen, alongside the Clean Fifteen, which highlights the fifteen produce items with the least pesticide residues.

The Dirty Dozen	
The 2024 Dirty Dozen includes these fruits and vegetables, which are recommended to be purchased organic due to their higher pesticide levels	
- Strawberries	- Bell and Hot Peppers
- Spinach	- Cherries
- Kale, Collard, and Mustard Greens	- Peaches
- Nectarines	- Pears
- Apples	- Celery
- Grapes	- Tomatoes
Note: The Dirty Dozen list also includes collard greens and hot peppers because they tend to contain significant levels of hazardous pesticides.	

The Clean Fifteen	
The Clean Fifteen list for 2024 features produce with the lowest pesticide residues, making them safer to buy non-organic	
- Avocados	- Honeydew Melons
- Sweet Corn	- Kiwis
- Pineapples	- Cabbages
- Onions	- Mushrooms
- Papayas	- Cantaloupes
- Sweet Peas (Frozen)	- Mangos
- Asparagus	- Watermelons
	- Sweet Potatoes
Note: Some sweet corn in the United States is genetically modified (GE). To avoid GE produce, choose organic varieties.	

APPENDIX 3

RECIPES INDEX

Made in United States
Troutdale, OR
10/12/2024

23688235R00058